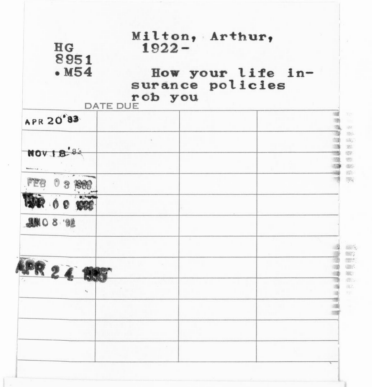

How
Your
Life
Insurance
Policies
Rob
You

ALSO BY ARTHUR MILTON

Life Insurance Stocks: The Modern Gold Rush
How to Get a Dollar's Value for a Dollar Spent
Life Insurance Stocks: An Investment Appraisal
Inflation: Everyone's Problem
Insurance Stocks: A Fortune to Share
Something More Can Be Done!
You Are Worth a Fortune
Will Inflation Destroy America?

ARTHUR MILTON

How
Your
Life
Insurance
Policies
Rob
You

CITADEL PRESS   SECAUCUS, N.J.

First printing

Libary of Congress Cataloging in Publication Data

Milton, Arthur, 1922-
    How your life insurance policies rob you.

    1. Insurance, Life—United States.   I. Title.
HG8951.M54   368.3′2′00973   81-4679
ISBN 0-8065-0768-3   AACR2

Dedication

There is an inherent irony in that the phrase life insurance actually represents a means of preparing for death. It's one way to make certain outstanding loans or unsettled business agreements are favorably resolved. And most important, it can protect a family when—in the natural order of things—the head of the household is no longer there to care for them.

And it is bitterly ironic that, as I was writing this book, I had to confront this subject head-on—not the death of a father or mother, or uncle, or brother, but the death of my youngest daughter, Patricia Ann.

It is to Pat I dedicate this book. To Pat, who loved life and all living things—who "collected" unwanted animals and neglected children, and captivated all who knew her with her loving spirit and generous heart.

When Pat died on May 7, 1980, at the age of 23, I realized a somber truth: You can protect your family for all the tomorrows through financial security, but the greatest legacy is your time and your love today . . . and each day that you live.

Above all, those were the gifts I wanted to leave my Patricia. As it happened, things did not happen in their natural order. With Patricia's untimely death these gifts were, instead, her legacy to me.

I am a far richer man for them.

IT IS THE AUTHOR'S INTENTION TO DONATE THE ROYALTIES RECEIVED FROM THE PUBLISHER OF THIS BOOK TO CHARITIES OR EDUCATIONAL ORGANIZATIONS IN MEMORY OF HIS DAUGHTER, PATRICIA ANN MILTON.

Acknowledgments

I am grateful:

To my associates, whose individual and collective capabilities enable me to find the time to speak out on the issues of our times.

To my many friends in insurance and the other professions, who over the years have contributed to my knowledge, views, enthusiasm, and philosophies.

To my clients, who have taught me much about human wants, needs, and behavior.

A. M.

Contents

9

business is on a "self-destruct course." This document is a tacit confession that the life companies long have grossly overcharged their customers.

5. Typical Abuses / 75

A typical life-insurance story and high-pressure mail-order selling . . . Conglomerate bottom-line perils .   . Scare selling: Who needs cancer insurance?

6. Double Dipping in Credit Life / 85

One-third of the $2.5 billion to $3 billion annual premium collections on credit life insurance probably represents over-charges, and to add insult to injury, the borrowing consumer has to pay high interest on the premium. A fight looms in Congress to end this abuse.

7. A Smug Industry / 93

Insurance companies are not public spirited. . . . They do little for policyholders hurt by inflation. . . . They drag their feet on accident prevention, crime, educational advancement, and other social issues.

8. The Heavy Grip of Inflation / 103

Inflation is warping and eroding the traditional concept of life insurance for many consumers. It could force changes in the product line and company structure that would wipe out the present agency system, force some life companies out of business, and compel the survivors to trim their sails and drastically change their way of doing business.

Preface

THIS BOOK WAS WRITTEN IN ANGER, an anger accumulated gradually over thirty-six years as a practicing insurance agent, insurance broker, and stock broker trading principally in insurance-company stocks.

Its purpose is to stir people to action on their own behalf and to help them gain financial security.

A secondary purpose is to generate debate in the insurance industry to cause action that will benefit our population, which is so dependent on insurance.

A large amount of information about the predatory, autocratic, and sometimes criminal activities of the life-insurance establishment is widely known to many persons active in the business and to some educators, regulatory officials, and politicians. I have remarked in previous books about some of the industry's greedy absurdities. Over the past twenty years, other authors and government reports have painted in the details of the ugly picture. The Institute of Life Insurance's 1974 *Trend Report,* circulated confidentially among the top brass of the industry establishment, admitted the truth of virtually all the accusations against the industry you will read about in this book. Of course, the *Trend Report* made these admissions in a very back-handed, self-righteous way, but the report reached the then-startling conclusion that the life-insurance industry was on a "self-destruct course" if it continued to operate as it has for the past century, with its huge emphasis on selling costly whole-life cash-value policies.

This conclusion, I am sure, was not reached without realizing that today even the life-insurance industry is dealing with a consumer movement that was nonexistent only 15 years ago. If the insurance industry doesn't act more vigorously and prudently to clean its house, consumerist leaders like Ralph Nader and Robert Hunter will do it for them. These two formed a new National Insurance Consumer Organization with considerable fanfare at a Washington meeting in October 1980. The education in recent years of our population, in money matters including insurance, cannot and should not be underestimated by the insurance industry and the regulators. In addition, the inflationary spiral has caused the average person to seek a dollar's value for a dollar spent even in buying death (life) insurance.

Getting back to the *Trend Report*—self-destruction for whom or for what? Certainly not for the basic principle of life insurance, which is financial protection for the survivors when a family breadwinner dies. Neither Americans nor any other people is going to give up that great social benefit achieved over the past two hundred and fifty years.

No, the self-destruction will be that of the predatory and hypocritical oligarchies who control and manage the establishment life-insurance companies, pursuing selfish, high-handed policies to delude millions of people and swindle them out of their earnings and savings. The impact of concentration of financial power in the life-insurance octopus on the national economy is evil and corrupting. Many life-insurance companies have corrupted representatives in Congress, many state legislators, and state regulatory officials in order to serve their privileged position and to keep the unsophisticated public from knowing about their duplicity and plundering.

Like most other insurance agents, I acquired this knowledge slowly. The first company I worked for gave me a training course that amounted to deliberate brainwashing. Necessarily, I sold some policies in my younger years I wouldn't dream of recommending today, but they were the best available to me then, just as wooden boats, which are subject to rot and require painting, caulking, and other costly maintenance, were the best available then to boat buyers. Now virtually all boats are made of fiberglass, which doesn't rot and requires virtually no maintenance. The establishment life companies have improved their products the way boat builders have, to meet the competition of the day. *They have not righted the longstanding wrongs to the older policyholders.*

But I am glad to say that I began opening my eyes rather early. I quickly realized the absurdity of such cruel hoaxes as the endowment policy, and I was still very young when I became outraged by the racial, religious, and sex discrimination toward both applicants for insurance and job hunters of the establishment companies. I was a pioneer in crying out against the folly of selling burdensome cash-value insurance to young people instead of inexpensive term insurance that provides genuine protection to survivors. But it took me longer to accept the fact that, in spite of all the benefits life insurance has conferred, the industry establishment has become a colossal monster that must be torn down and completely rebuilt. For example, the waste of policyholders' money not only on inflated salaries, but on grandiose architecture for home offices to feed the egos of top management, should be relegated to the past.

I was not alone in the industry in rebelling against its abuses and injustices. A number of other life-insurance executives and agents and some regulators of the industry have spoken out over the years against the abuses and excesses complained of in this book. These courageous people will not regret the appearance of this book, because its indictment does not pertain to them. Some of them have had to pay with their jobs for their efforts to bring out the truth, but they have persisted. This kind of criticism from within the profession is needed more than ever today by the insuring public.

So, like the case with many other economic and social abuses, the individual American is not helpless in the face of the sins of the life-insurance establishment. If he or she will take some time to study the matter, enough companies can be found that are eager to sell death protection at reasonable cost and on fair terms, and there are enough independent agents with sufficient sophistication and integrity to help them—companies and agents who foresee the future in this age of consumerism and want to serve the policy buyer, not swindle her or him.

But what about the tens of millions who are too unsophisticated and too apathetic to mend matters on their own? Should the life-insurance predators continue to be allowed to gouge them mercilessly? No!

I can only hope that the two hundred thousand-plus captive life-insurance agents in America are becoming as sensible and sensitive as I have become to the injustices of the establishment companies. But I suspect many of them will feel they would be risking their jobs by being caught with a copy of this book.

In any event, we certainly should not continue to tolerate the corruption and domination of so much of our economy and government by the greedy and arrogant ruling clique of the insurance establishment.

ARTHUR MILTON

Introduction

T HE ONLY THING THAT IS CONSTANT IS CHANGE.
This cliché is well-known by those who recognize that decade
after decade the progress of our country and the progress of
our world have often meant constant change, particularly in
the sphere of economics as it pertains to each and every individual. Frankly, for decades I have felt that the term *life
insurance* is a misnomer. I now feel the time has come to do
away with this misnomer and call it what it is, *death insurance.*

We call financial protection against flames fire insurance and protection against loss by overflowing streams flood
insurance, and the various parts of a comprehensive automobile insurance policy are known by the perils protected
against. So why not call protection against the hazard of
death by its right name? I suspect the misnomer *life insurance*
arose because of the dread of death and the taboo against
talking too much about it in an age more superstitious than
ours. But *life insurance* is an absurd label, and the term
living insurance being promoted by one large establishment
company is even more farfetched. (However, since *life insurance* is so widely used and is even part of the names of
many companies, I have used the term throughout this book,
to avoid confusion.)

People should protect their loved ones, and their business properties, and their outstanding loans, and their busi-

ness agreements, with proper death insurance, and the result should be maximum protection for minimum premium outlay. I have always felt that utilizing a so-called life-insurance policy as a savings vehicle was not a good investment. In this era of runaway inflation, in this era of high interest rates available to you on investments, it is absolutely absurd in most cases either to continue your cash-value life-insurance policies or to consider the purchase of new ones.

Also, the need for you to consider a much greater amount of death (life) insurance than you probably have is certainly clear.

Finally, after I have advised tens of thousands of clients over the past thirty-six years to purchase the right kind of insurance, consumer advocates, as well as many of those in the life-insurance industry, and particularly those in government, now have sided with my philosophy and theories on *financial planning*.

As you read through the following pages, you will find important information that makes it absolutely necessary for you to start an immediate review of your *death-insurance* needs and also to consider appropriate areas in which to invest your capital so that you may have adequate financial security in your twilight years.

1. *The Voracious Octopus*

W E AMERICANS are going through the most frustrating period of our national history since the Civil War, but there is one serious evil every one of us can help overcome.

We are encompassed by a sea of troubles, mostly of our own making but some resulting from the malice, envy, and bigoted fanaticism of other peoples throughout the world, peoples whom we have tried to befriend but have succeeded only in making into enemies. At home we are beset by a persistent serious inflation (13.4 percent in 1980) we have not been able to cope with, an energy crisis that is fairly certain to bring our standard of living down permanently, falling productivity in our industry, an apparent breakdown of much of our school system, appalling crime, and a moral and social convulsion most of us cannot even comprehend, much less cope with.

We have been humiliated in Iran, and our national con-

science over the war in Vietnam will be a continuing canker
to us for generations to come.

These frustrations are doubly bitter to the individual
American, because he or she can do nothing about any of
these terrible evils. Only concerted national opinion and action, guided by determined leadership, can have the slightest
effect.

The evil we all *can* do something about immediately has
been going on for a hundred and twenty-five years, and the
majority of Americans are extremely reluctant to recognize
it and wipe it out, although it has extracted from millions of
persons billions of dollars. It has cruelly hoaxed most of the
population and has created a predatory financial oligarchy,
the scale of whose deceptive and avaricious practices makes
those of organized crime, and of nearly all the other greedy
and oppressive commercial and industrial oligarchies of the
past, seem petty.

With thirty-six years of a close relationship I feel obligated to tell my readers my observations in the strongest
terms possible, as well as relating my concerns. Fortunately,
these broad-brush accusations apply to only a few. By and
large, those serving the insurance industry are honorable
persons and, I am convinced, can and will change the climate
for the betterment of our entire population, which is dependent on an honest insurance industry.

The perpetrators of this evil, which we all have the
ability to elude and erode if we will, are the most hypocritical
rascals ever seen in this country, with the possible exception
of the more scandalous religious charlatans of today and the
nineteenth-century patent-medicine barons. Today's charlatans are the life-insurance companies, who sell millions of
overpriced and almost useless cash-value policies to persons

who, instead, desperately need adequate, sensibly priced financial protection for the survivors when the family breadwinner dies.

The reluctance of the American public to accept the fact that the life-insurance establishment has been operating a monstrous and cruel racket for generations is natural enough. People think about life insurance with gratitude because it did provide a means, albeit a grossly inadequate means, of fending off starvation and homelessness, in the wake of the vast social upheaval caused by the industrial revolution and the military and political revolutions that accompanied it.

Although the life-insurance industry is nearly two hundred and fifty years old, it grew very slowly in the first century for two fairly obvious reasons. To many millions it seemed an unfeasible idea because human life then was so uncertain and mortality rates were so high. This made it an unattractive business to the hardheaded eighteenth-century and early-nineteenth-century financiers. The other reason was that it seemed unnecessary in an age when society in much of the world, even in the industrialized countries, was still stratified and feudal and most people had a place tied in some way to the land. People had roots in the land on which they could depend. The nobility and the rich landholders were obligated by law, custom, and religion to care for the widow and children of a tenant, serf, or employee who died. They had to make a place for these dependents and give them at least the bare necessities of life. Therefore the populace, which was semiliterate at best, was slow to apprecaite the idea of life insurance.

The erosion of feudalism in England began in Tudor times, with the first enclosure movements that drove some peasants off the lands their forebears had farmed for genera-

tions. The industrial revolution and the new enclosure movements in England and Scotland in the eighteenth century,
when landlords uprooted hundreds of thousands of tenants
and sharecroppers to make room for sheep grazing, finished
off the remnants of British feudalism. The same thing happened on the Continent of Europe. The world's millions became indeed the world's dispossessed. They no longer had
roots and a place on the land to which they had a hereditary
right to return or a lord or landlord who owed them succor.

Life insurance began to make sense. But it still was not
easy to sell, and it was even more difficult to get insured
persons to keep up their policies and pay premiums. Also, in
both Europe and the United States, the young industry encountered many frauds on the part of applicants for insurance. Medical examinations were falsified, and insured
persons, particularly children, were murdered in large numbers to collect on the policies. In an age when most parents
could reasonably expect two out of five or even more of their
offspring to die of childhood maladies, an astonishing number
of couples saw nothing wrong in exploiting this fact to de-
fraud the insurance companies. So, historically speaking at
least, not all the wrong has been on the part of the companies.
But the life-insurance companies responded to these abuses
by writing tough, even very tricky clauses into the policies
designed to prevent fraud by insured persons and their beneficiaries. Indeed, they put in so many restrictive clauses that
the business began to get a bad reputation, and selling policies became even more difficult.

Then someone thought of cash value, realizing that this
"savings" feature could become a most potent sales tool, a
great inducement to insured persons to keep up their policies,
and an excuse for raising premiums sharply. It is doubtful

that the insurance men who first launched the cash-value policy realized what an enormous bonanza it would turn out to be by increasing the sales volume of high-priced whole-life policies to a golden flood. But it wasn't long before smart financiers saw the immense possibilities, got into the business, and began to milk the public—and they have been doing it ever since.

So we see that cash values were not a part of the original life-insurance concept; in fact, very soon after they were introduced, thoughtful critics began to condemn the whole idea. The first published criticism appeared in the United States in 1868. The critics pointed out that cash values did nothing but raise the cost of death protection for the insured's survivors. They also saw correctly that the so-called savings feature of cash value in life-insurance policies was a hoax because the savings were not added to the death benefit and, in the long run, rarely amounted to nearly as much as the policyholders had paid in.

Even at that early date and in that era of relatively low interest rates and stable currencies, sober voices were raised warning the public that the only real function of life insurance was the financial protection of survivors and that life insurance never could be anything but an inferior investment instrument.

Although whole-life insurance was the original concept, sophisticated buyers with high purchasing power were rather quick to see how expensive it really was. Ultimately these sophisticates negotiated deals for large amounts of life insurance on fixed, renewable terms at greatly reduced premium prices that went up with each renewal. But few companies got into this business, and those which did kept it so in the dark that their own agents did not know about it for

TABLE OF MORTALITY

Death Rates per 1,000 and Expectation of Life

Based on the Commissioners 1958 Standard Ordinary (C.S.O.) Mortality Table

Age	Number Living	Deaths each Year	Deaths per 1000	Expectation of Life	Age	Number Living	Deaths each Year	Deaths per 1000	Expectation of Life
1	1,000,000	1,760	1.76	67.78	51	875,134	7,972	9.11	22.82
2	998,240	1,517	1.52	66.90	52	867,162	8,637	9.96	22.03
3	996,723	1,455	1.46	66.00	53	858,525	9,349	10.89	21.25
4	995,268	1,393	1.40	65.10	54	849,176	10,105	11.90	20.47
5	993,875	1,342	1.35	64.19	55	839,071	10,908	13.00	19.71
6	992,533	1,290	1.30	63.27	56	828,163	11,768	14.21	18.97
7	991,243	1,249	1.26	62.35	57	816,395	12,687	15.54	18.23
8	989,994	1,218	1.23	61.43	58	803,708	13,663	17.00	17.51
9	988,776	1,196	1.21	60.51	59	790,045	14,687	18.59	16.81
10	987,580	1,195	1.21	59.58	60	775,358	15,771	20.34	16.12
11	986,385	1,212	1.23	58.65	61	759,587	16,893	22.24	15.44
12	985,172	1,241	1.26	57.72	62	742,694	18,055	24.31	14.78
13	983,931	1,299	1.32	56.80	63	724,639	19,254	26.57	14.14
14	982,632	1,366	1.39	55.87	64	705,385	20,484	29.04	13.51
15	981,266	1,433	1.46	54.95	65	684,901	21,746	31.75	12.90
16	979,833	1,509	1.54	54.03	66	663,155	23,038	34.74	12.31
17	978,324	1,585	1.62	53.11	67	640,117	24,350	38.04	11.73
18	976,739	1,651	1.69	52.19	68	615,767	25,665	41.68	11.17
19	975,088	1,697	1.74	51.28	69	590,102	26,915	45.61	10.64
20	973,391	1,742	1.79	50.37	70	563,187	28,041	49.79	10.12
21	971,649	1,778	1.83	49.46	71	535,146	28,978	54.15	9.63
22	969,871	1,804	1.86	48.55	72	506,168	29,687	58.65	9.15
23	968,067	1,830	1.89	47.64	73	476,481	30,142	63.26	8.69
24	966,237	1,846	1.91	46.73	74	446,339	30,405	68.12	8.24
25	964,391	1,861	1.93	45.82	75	415,934	30,517	73.37	7.81

Age	Number Living	Deaths each Year	Deaths per 1000	Expectation of Life	Age	Number Living	Deaths each Year	Deaths per 1000	Expectation of Life
26	962,530	1,887	1.96	44.90	76	385,417	30,517	79.18	7.39
27	960,643	1,912	1.99	43.99	77	354,900	30,415	85.70	6.98
28	958,731	1,946	2.03	43.08	78	324,485	30,197	93.06	6.59
29	956,785	1,990	2.08	42.16	79	294,288	29,779	101.19	6.21
30	954,795	2,034	2.13	41.24	80	264,509	29,091	109.98	5.85
31	952,764	2,087	2.19	40.34	81	235,418	28,097	119.35	5.51
32	950,674	2,139	2.25	39.43	82	207,321	26,780	129.17	5.19
33	948,535	2,201	2.32	38.51	83	180,541	25,164	139.38	4.89
34	946,334	2,271	2.40	37.60	84	155,377	23,308	150.01	4.60
35	944,063	2,370	2.51	36.69	85	132,069	21,282	161.14	4.32
36	941,693	2,486	2.64	35.78	86	110,787	19,146	172.82	4.06
37	939,207	2,630	2.80	34.88	87	91,641	16,965	185.13	3.80
38	936,577	2,819	3.01	33.97	88	74,676	14,805	198.25	3.55
39	933,758	3,035	3.25	33.07	89	59,871	12,720	212.46	3.31
40	930,723	3,285	3.53	32.18	90	47,151	10,757	228.14	3.06
41	927,438	3,561	3.84	31.29	91	36,394	8,945	245.77	2.82
42	923,877	3,853	4.17	30.41	92	27,449	7,300	265.93	2.58
43	920,024	4,168	4.53	29.54	93	20,149	5,829	289.30	2.33
44	915,856	4,506	4.92	28.67	94	14,320	4,535	316.66	2.07
45	911,350	4,876	5.35	27.81	95	9,785	3,437	351.24	1.80
46	906,474	5,285	5.83	26.95	96	6,348	2,543	400.56	1.51
47	901,189	5,732	6.36	26.11	97	3,805	1,858	488.42	1.18
48	895,457	6,223	6.95	25.27	98	1,947	1,301	668.15	.83
49	889,234	6,758	7.60	24.45	99	646	646	1,000.00	.50
50	882,476	7,342	8.32	23.63					

many years. So much pressure was exerted on agents to keep this term-insurance business secret that it was almost never mentioned in public.

So for more than a century, enormous pressure was put on insurance agents to concentrate on selling expensive cash-value policies. This pressure continues virtually unabated today. It was achieved mainly by making the commission schedule on cash-value insurance so much more attractive than the commissions on term insurance that many agents felt they could not afford to recommend modestly priced term insurance to customers. Indeed, for a long time the agents were so ill-trained and so rigorously indoctrinated that millions of them took as gospel the representations of the companies that whole life and cash value were what was really best for their customers. The average "captive" agent who represented only one company appeared to have an evangelical faith in whatever the company told him—what was best for the company was obviously what was best for humankind. Many still have that faith—or pretend to.

It takes only a minute's reflection to understand why cash-value insurance has to be overpriced and provide vastly less protection than term insurance. Fundamentally, an insurance company, when it writes a policy, makes a wager that the insured will not die soon. The odds for this wager are set on the basis of tables of mortality experience.* The younger the policy buyer is, the longer odds the company can afford to give in the form of low premiums; the older the policy buyer, the shorter the odds and the higher the premiums. Whole-life insurance policies have an element not found in any other usual type of wager: Every one of us must

---

* See Mortality Table, page 26.

die eventually, so the insurance company must pay the bet—unless the policy lapses. As a matter of fact, a very high percentage of whole life policies do lapse, and the company gets whatever has been paid in premiums and the policyholder loses his or her wager outright. Unlike the horse-racing bookmakers and other professional gamblers who take wagers from the public, the life companies calculate their odds so they make money on virtually every individual policy even though they have to pay off a great many of their wagers. The only time the company loses is when an insured person dies soon after taking out the policy. But even these losses are much more than offset by the large number of policies that lapse. On these, no death benefit ever has to be paid.

In practice, rates have been set higher than really was necessary, so the difference between the cost of term insurance in the younger and middle years and of whole life insurance is staggering. The harsh truth is that the average family can buy from five to ten times as much insurance protection for

ANNUAL PREMIUMS FOR $100,000

Age	Yearly Renewable-Term	vs	Cash-Value Whole-Life
21	$ 153.00		$ 898.00
22	153.00		918.00
23	154.00		942.00
24	155.00		971.00
25	156.00		1,005.00
26	158.00		1,045.00
27	161.00		1,088.00
28	165.00		1,135.00
29	168.00		1,185.00
30	172.00		1,240.00
31	175.00		1,296.00
32	178.00		1,353.00
33	182.00		1,408.00
34	187.00		1,467.00

ANNUAL PREMIUMS FOR $100,000 (*Continued*)

Age	Yearly Renewable-Term	vs	Cash-Value Whole-Life
35	192.00		1,530.00
36	205.00		1,589.00
37	221.00		1,658.00
38	238.00		1,737.00
39	257.00		1,826.00
40	279.00		1,925.00
41	300.00		2,008.00
42	321.00		2,101.00
43	346.00		2,204.00
44	376.00		2,417.00
45	407.00		2,440.00
46	454.00		2,556.00
47	503.00		2,682.00
48	556.00		2,818.00
49	613.00		2,964.00
50	671.00		3,120.00
51	727.00		3,302.00
52	784.00		3,494.00
53	845.00		3,696.00
54	914.00		3,908.00
55	995.00		4,130.00
56	1,086.00		4,355.00
57	1,185.00		4,595.00
58	1,296.00		4,855.00
59	1,420.00		5,135.00
60	1,559.00		5,435.00
61	1,710.00		5,750.00
62	1,874.00		6,085.00
63	2,054.00		6,445.00
64	2,257.00		6,830.00
65	2,485.00		7,245.00

The above premiums are typical of policies issued by a stock life-insurance company

a dollar in term policies as in whole-life cash-value insurance. Life rates are complicated, depending on many factors such as age, health, the amount of insurance bought, various policy options, and the term of the policy. Thus, there is a wide range in the amounts of term and whole-life insurance a dollar will buy.

It is axiomatic that the bigger the unit prices and markups of what it sells, the more profitable an efficiently run business is in terms of percentage return on sales. This is the basic profit bonanza the establishment life-insurance industry has succeeded in building and maintaining for a century in the United States and Europe.

For many years the establishment companies were not satisfied with even these huge premium profits. So they introduced a hybrid called the endowment policy and sold it as if it were manna from heaven. This was a deal under which the sucker paid on the policy for twenty, thirty, or forty years, then could cash it in for a little better amount than the cash value of whole life or trade it for a small annuity payable until death. The trouble with this little beauty was that it provided only one-thirtieth to one-tenth as much death protection for the money as term insurance.

Life-insurance companies take the money you pay in premiums and invest it in stocks and bonds or lend it. They reap rather handsome profits on these investments for many years. The income is kept on the books in a separate account from premium income, but it all goes toward the overall profit on the company's shares if it is a stock company. Many of the big establishment life companies are mutuals. In theory, they are owned by their policyholders and pay dividends on the policies instead of dividends on stock. Most critics of the mutual companies contend that these dividends are in the main only a return of a small amount of the excessive premiums the mutual companies charge on whole-life policies, sometimes as much as thirty percent more than the charges of stock life companies. The U.S. Internal Revenue Service apparently agrees with this position. It never has sought to tax the dividends on mutual life-insurance policies as profit or income. Neither does the government tax the

policy dividends paid on "participating" policies issued by
stock life-insurance companies. It taxes only dividends paid
directly on their shares.

In general, the life companies have historically had
excellent returns on invested capital as well as high returns
on sales. Until the mid-1960s, there were many instances in
which you could have invested as little as ten thousand dollars
in a life company, and it would have appreciated through
stock splits and stock dividends until the original ten thousand dollars had become perhaps five hundred thousand dollars.* However, the life-insurance-stock market peaked in
1964, and there have been fewer bonanzas in recent years.
Still, life insurance is far from a capital-intensive business.
It runs on money collected from policyholders and its investments, not on the sale of new securities or borrowings, as
other businesses do. The big multi-line companies do have a
lot of stock in the hands of the public, but much of it was
issued as stock dividends or to pay for the purchase of other
insurance businesses. Very little was sold for cash.

Nevertheless, most life-insurance companies have big
sales volumes in proportion to their invested capital. So when
they reap a high yield on policy premiums and a high yield
on capital they are profiting doubly at the expense of the
public—to a degree that few businesses have been able to do
without resorting to monopolistic practices. The truth is that
most businesses that have high sales volumes in proportion to
invested capital—supermarket chains, for example—have to
content themselves with very small yields on sales, perhaps

---

* See Arthur Milton, *Life Insurance Stocks: The Modern Gold Rush* (Secaucus, N.J.: Citadel Press, 1963)'.

only two percent, and be satisfied with a respectable yield on capital. If such businesses seek too high a yield on sales they become uncompetitive.

Like policy dividends, the cash-value accumulations under whole-life insurance policies are not profit, although many insurance agents pretend they are and the companies do little to dispel the illusion. Again the proof that these accumulations are not profit but only a partial repayment to the policyholder of the excessive premium he or she has been charged is that the Internal Revenue Service has so ruled and never has sought to tax cash-value payments as profit or even as income. A warning: If cash surrender values and dividends eventually exceed the total amount of premiums paid in over the years, the excess can become taxable income. This sometimes happens.

By now some readers may imagine I want Congress to outlaw cash-value life policies and the courts to start sending insurance-company executives and agents to jail for selling them. Perish the thought!

It is the gross abuse of whole-life cash-value insurance that arouses my ire, not the principle itself. In fact, I still believe firmly that there are instances in which whole-life cash-value insurance is the only solution. The great weakness of term insurance is that one might be refused renewal of term policies on health grounds if the wrong term policy is purchased. Term insurance for periods of time such as one year, five years, or more can be purchased so that the policy is renewable and convertible without further medical examination. There are companies, however, that sell term insurance, without the renewable, convertible feature, at somewhat lower premiums. Except in rare instances, I don't think the premium savings is worth risking the loss of these two features.

Even though term insurance provides vastly more death protection for young people while they are rearing their children than a cash-value policy, comparisons between the two get somewhat complicated and even difficult over a long period. The reason is that the life-insurance market is confused to the point of chaos. The wide range in the prices of policies between well-run and badly run or deliberately predatory companies is almost incredible. There can be variations of almost a hundred percent in the pricing of identical policies.

Thus, it is possible to find a modestly priced, dividend-paying whole-life cash-value policy that will provide death protection more cheaply in the long run than a level death-benefit term policy for the same amount at the same age in a high-priced company. This contradiction is much stressed in the sales pitches of the establishment companies, but it really only underlines the need to get the help of a competent, reliable independent agent in buying any life insurance. Also the financial comparisons usually presented in support of such claims for whole-life insurance are hard for the lay person to comprehend and are based on dividend assumptions that are only guesses, since the dividends are not guaranteed. They are also based on the assumption that if the policyholder invested the excess amount of premium in something else, the interest rate she or he would receive would be very low.

Whole-life policies are widely used in the special field of business life insurance, which includes partnership insurance and key-man protection. A partnership policy protects the surviving partner or partners from the financially unpleasant consequences of the death of one partner. Key-man insurance provides money to tide a business over the trying days following the death of its active head or any other key people. Whole-life insurance has been sold in this field by agents who make big commissions on it on the plea that it alone can meet high health risks in business—for example, a heart attack striking a partner—and that renewing term insurance in such circumstances would be difficult or at least very expensive. The argument is also advanced that cash values are useful in business life insurance because there is always the possibility that something might happen that would make it desirable to terminate the insurance and recover some of the premium. However, many insurance people believe that judicious use of the right kind of term insurance can be cheaper and just as efficient in solving business-life-insurance problems.

For a few persons in high tax brackets, whole-life insurance with cash value is useful under the so-called minimum-deposit, or financed-life-insurance, plan. This involves buying a dividend-paying whole-life policy, then, after paying the premium in full four out of the first seven years under a special requirement of the IRS code, borrowing out the cash values. The assumption is that tax-exempt policy dividends will reduce the cost of the death protection below what term insurance could cost, while the interest paid on the borrowed-out cash values is also tax deductible. Many experts believe, though, that minimum-deposit life insurance rests on too many risky premises and that in practice, greedy agents too often have sold it to persons not really in a position to profit by it.

Of course, the galloping inflation that has engulfed the American economy in recent years has forced us all to face up to the consequences of the whole-life ripoff. Inflation has eroded the prospective death benefit of the small whole-life policy we bought many years ago until it hardly seems worthwhile to continue to pay premiums on it. Wouldn't it be better to cash it in and put the money in a savings bank or in some other investment that pays reasonably good interest or in stock that pays dividends? *

This situation has created a problem for the insurance industry, a problem the life-insurance trade press calls "the replacement crisis." Many insurance agents are either persuading their customers to replace their old policies with newer ones that offer more protection and better cash and dividend values—or with packages of term insurance and such outright investment instruments as annuities—or they are yielding to the customer's pleas for such help. This sort of thing flies right in the face of the philosophy of the establishment companies. It is plain heresy, and they are filling the insurance trade press and the general press, when they can, with exhortations to people to hang on to their old policies no matter how bad they are. Also, it comes as rank insubordination on the part of the agents; how dare these upstarts put their customers' needs ahead of the sacred privileges of the establishment fat cats?

Writing in the *National Underwriter* for December 1, 1979, Richard K. Carter, a vice-president of New York Life Insurance Company, quoted Calvin Coolidge, whose penny-pinching and ever-backward-looking policies brought on the great depression of the 1930s, as urging people in a radio talk in 1931 not to let anyone persuade them to switch their policies "without the best advice of the companies that issued them. . . . If you let someone switch you, he will surely make

*See Arthur Milton, *Will Inflation Destroy America?* (Secaucus, N.J.: Citadel Press, 1977).

money, but you will probably lose." Cautious Cal was a director of New York Life at the time. Carter opined that Coolidge's remarks were valid for today.

Hogwash! The American people are starting to disagree most emphatically.

To life-insurance people, one of the most criminal aspects of the current inflation is that, in effect, it makes life insurance seem worthless to persons in their late sixties or seventies unless they are quite well off. Most ordinary folk that old cannot afford the high premiums of term insurance in those brackets even if they are still physically insurable, and the whole-life policies they bought years ago have been rendered almost worthless by inflation. The death benefit of many of these policies won't exceed six months' or a year's Social Security benefits. A really small whole-life policy may not even pay for a decent funeral. Social Security provides a burial benefit, but it isn't much.

The revolt against whole-life cash-value insurance abuses is already well advanced. The industry's approximate figures show that fifty-two percent of the $407 billion worth of new individual life insurance sold in 1978 was term, not whole life. The American people and the independent agents have forced this change. But the greater part of the term insurance still is not written by the big establishment companies or even by the many smaller conventional companies. It is written by companies formed to write such business and a few older companies that have seen the wave of the future.

That fifty-two-percent figure doesn't mean that the struggle is won or is necessarily going to be won without a big effort. The greater amount of premium income in the business, and particularly the premium income of the establishment companies, comes from whole-life cash-value insurance by far, and that's the way the establishment companies want to keep things. *What is being bought today does not offset the bad impact on the public of the costly cash values or even high-cost term policies sold in the past.*

Milwaukee insurance man Aaron Zelman, one of the authors of *Life Insurance Conspiracy,** points out another reason why the fifty-two-percent figure for term insurance's share of the total market in 1978 should be put in perspective and taken with a grain of salt. Zelman says that many of the big establishment companies will not sell a term policy of less than fifty thousand dollars, and most of their policies are much bigger. This inflates the statistical share of term insurance in their volume, but the fifty-thousand-dollar floor is further evidence of their determination to keep the family on a modest income shackled to costly whole-life insurance.

The sins of the establishment life companies do not end with abuse of whole-life cash-value policies. Throughout much of the industry's history they have operated on outdated mortality tables that enable them to inflate their rates and rig the odds of their insurance wagers in favor of the companies and against policyholders and their beneficiaries.

For years they discriminated against women and racial minorities unconscionably, penalizing females unjustly and outrightly denying insurance to blacks. They rule their captive agents with a tyrannical hand and have brought extreme pressure against independent agents to prevent the dissemination of information about the realities of life-insurance economics and to preserve the fictitious gospel that their predatory policies are necessary and just.

* Peter Spielman and Aaron Zelman, *The Life Insurance Conspiracy: Made Simple by Holmes and Watson* (New York: Simon and Schuster, Inc., 1976).

The companies have also achieved enormous financial power: They became as potent as the banking establishment as a source of funds for equity and loan capital for business and other segments of the national economy. They used this financial power ruthlessly, to influence legislators and regulatory officials so the companies can protect their selfish interests. Thus, this voracious octopus spreads its tentacles ever wider, to suck blood and treasure from the American people. They even succeeded in getting amendments tacked onto federal laws, forbidding some government agencies to oppose their ruthless policies.

I am chagrined and even embarrassed at many of my colleagues who are behaving in such an unprofessional manner—after all, they will have to accede eventually to the current needs of the people they serve. I am concerned that the many insurance associations that I have been a member of for thirty-six years cannot see the forest for the trees in this ever-changing world.

Nevertheless, in the long run, the life-insurance establishment was not able to prevent sensibly priced term insurance from being made available to the general public through independent companies and independent agents. Since about 1950, sensible, reasonably priced term insurance has been available.

That has not stopped these big companies and their armies of agents from continuing to mislead the public and sell people unsuitable policies at high prices. It has not stopped their flood of false propaganda about the great virtues of cash-value insurance, and it has not stopped their effort to prevent or delay the spread of truthful information about life-insurance economics.

The confused situation is aggravated by the attitude of

the establishment life companies that anyone outside their own official family who presumes to write or talk about life insurance is guilty of prejudice and ignorance and is telling malicious lies in an effort to tear down a sacred institution. They are particularly incensed when members of Congress such as Senator Howard Metzenbaum, government bodies such as the Federal Trade Commission, or academic economists specializing in insurance present caustic analytical pictures of the industry and its products. They accuse the critics of having political or at least self-serving motives.

Considering all the political shenanigans that many investigations in our national history have revealed on the part of the establishment life-insurance companies, and considering the huge lobbies they maintain in Washington and every state capital, it is downright comical for the insurance establishment to call the FTC and the academic economists politically biased and self-serving.

Just what can individual Americans do to overcome the voracious life-insurance octopus? The answer is simple: Just be very careful about buying life insurance. Find out about it. Information is available. Ever since Herbert Denenberg (who moved from a professorship at the University of Pennsylvania's Wharton School to become the state's insurance commissioner) published *The Shopper's Guide to Life Insurance* and circulated two million copies of it, eye-opening information has been available. Denenberg bluntly urged Congress to outlaw cash-value life insurance unless the companies came up with an honest and adequate program of pricing-information disclosure. He also charged that eighty percent of the companies were "suspect" and that forty percent of all agents were incompetent.

In the years since the first appearance of the Denenberg

guide, New York and several other states have published similar guides. So it is manifest that no one has to be victimized by a life-insurance company any longer.

However, no matter how honestly and carefully they are prepared, these official guides to buying life insurance are not easy reading. It takes a lot of time and a natural aptitude or long experience at research to digest them. Articles in such publications as *Changing Times* and consumer magazines stick more to general principles with fewer cumbersome details, but they still leave the uninitiated pretty puzzled.

In other words, you still need an agent. The question is, What kind of agent? Here are some rules for choosing one:

• Don't select an agent just because he or she is a relative or neighbor. Check the agent for competence. Don't regard a big sales volume as the prime indicator—that could indicate just an unscrupulous huckster.

• If you choose a captive agent who works for a single company, make sure you buy the kind of policy you need and want, not the policy the company wants him or her to sell. Captive agents may be honest and friendly, but you are likely to find their services more useful for fire, automobile, and other property and casualty insurance than for death protection, if they work for a multiline company. That's what they most likely have learned best.

• If you choose an independent agent you still have to check him or her out carefully. If the agent seems in a hurry to get your check and signature on the application, show him or her the door and look for someone more interested in your personal needs. Independent agents generally do not work for a single company. They also sell all kinds of insurance and annuities, and fortunately for you, they do not have to make a *maximum* commission on a sale of life insurance that's unsuited for you.

The New York State Insurance Department gives these additional rules:

• Check whether the agent is a full-timer or just sells insurance as a sideline.
• Ask friends, relatives, and business associates to recommend agents.
• Make sure the agent you select really has specialized education and training in both insurance and allied financial-planning fields.
• Talk with him or her. If you don't feel that an agent cares about your personal needs, find another one.
• Make sure an agent explains the costs and coverage of everything fully.
• Try to decide if he or she is the kind of person you can depend on to keep you posted about changes in available coverages and other opportunities. A lazy agent can really hurt you.
• Make sure she or he isn't the kind of ripoff artist who, under the pretext of reviewing your situation, will sell you new policies no better than those you have, just to generate commissions.

Even these fairly simple rules aren't easy to follow, but I can give you one rule that is easy to follow, and since most persons buying death insurance for the first or second time are relatively young, it applies to most people. Here it is:

Life insurance is really death insurance. The first consideration in buying it, the only real consideration, is to pro-

vide maximum financial protection for surviving family members if the breadwinner is killed or dies of illness. In these days when both husband and wife often have jobs, such protection may be needed against the death of both spouses. A survivor of either sex is in a devil of a spot today if he or she loses a spouse and has children to bring up.

The basic rule is, truly, maximum dollar protection for minimum cost.

2. *Time for Federal Intervention*

FOR TWO AND A HALF YEARS, the Federal Trade Commission wrestled with the problem of working out a better way to show consumers how to find out just how good or bad a life insurance policy is.

The long effort resulted in a 455-page report published in the midsummer of 1979. Its conclusions startled, even stunned, people who didn't know much about life insurance and enraged some industry leaders. The report said that the average return to policyholders on whole-life cash-value insurance was only 1.3 percent in 1977. The FTC staff added that life-insurance-policy holders would have received $3.7 billion more that year if the companies had paid them a reasonable yield on their policies, which the commission estimated would have been 4 percent.

The report said that most persons who bought nonparticipating cash-value whole-life policies—that is, policies that don't pay dividends—in the 1950s and 1960s would do well to cash them in now and either buy term insurance or new dividend-paying whole-life policies with much better yields.

The big emphasis in the report, however, was on a demand for much stricter disclosure in advance of the true cost of policies and the true yields and dividends over various periods of time on the different types of policies.

Chairman Michael Pertshuk of the FTC made perhaps the most damning comment. Pertshuk said, "No other product in our economy that is purchased by so many people for so much money is bought with so little understanding of its actual or comparative value."

The reaction to the FTC staff report, from both the public and the life-insurance industry, was explosive. All over the country people reading about it in the press or hearing about it on radio or television began calling or writing their insurance agents and brusquely ordering them to cash in whole-life policies they had been paying on for years and write cheap term insurance instead.

A number of small insurance companies and independent agents began advertising term insurance or new comparatively high-yield, dividend-paying whole-life policies to replace old policies. This created a lot of turmoil. There are laws and formalities that must be observed by agents in changing an insured person's life policies. (See chapter 10.)

Of course, the establishment companies and their trade associations denounced the FTC staff report. They said that it prejudged the issues, manipulated statistics, buried legitimate information favorable to older whole-life cash-value insurance, and confused the public and that generally speaking, the FTC staff showed a totally unjustifiable bias in favor of term insurance against whole-life insurance.

A publication of the American Society of Chartered Life

Underwriters called the staff report "an inexcusable and apparently deliberate effort to destroy public confidence in the life insurance business."

President Blake Newton of the American Council of Life Insurance (successor to the old Institute of Life Insurance) and the council's chairman, Armand C. Stalnaker, who is also chairman of General American Life Insurance Company, have been making speeches and giving interviews denouncing the FTC staff report.

More significantly, in November 1979, the life companies succeeded in getting the Senate Commerce Committee to approve the Cannon Insurance Amendment to the Federal Trade Commission Act. Reporting on this vote, the December 1979 issue of the *Bulletin of the Life Underwriters Association of the City of New York* said that the Cannon Amendment "would make it clear that the FTC does not have the authority under McCarran-Ferguson Act to investigate the business of life insurance."

The McCarran-Ferguson Act, passed in 1945, reaffirmed the life-insurance companies' exemption from the federal antitrust laws, on the ground that the companies are adequately regulated by the states.

The significance of this vote is put in focus by the following editorial published by the *New York Times* on July 27, 1979, before the commttee acted.

THE WHOLE TRUTH ABOUT LIFE INSURANCE

Would you put your money in a savings account paying 1.3 percent interest? According to a new Federal Trade Commission report, that's just about what many Americans do in purchasing life insurance. Life insurance companies hold more than $140 billion of the public's savings—roughly the amount held in passbook savings and loan association accounts—and generally pay returns far below the rate available in equally secure investments. The only plausible explanation is that policyholders don't realize how raw a deal they are getting. By the Commission's reckoning and ours, the most sensible solution is tough disclosure rules for life insurance companies.

The problem concerns "whole" life insurance. That is the most popular form involving savings as well as insurance. In 1977 about half of every insurance dollar was used to pay for death benefits and company expenses. The rest was socked away in insurance company investments on behalf of the policyholders or returned to them as dividends.

The holders of some of the policies examined by the Federal Trade Commission were paid a return, on the investment portion of their premiums, that was comparable to what they could have earned in the bank. But most policies, particularly those first written in the 1950's and early 1960's, paid far less. And virtually every purchaser of whole life insurance who allowed the policy to lapse within five years earned no interest at all.

Buyers can, of course, avoid the problem by avoiding whole life insurance and putting their savings in a bank. However, if people insist on buying whole life insurance—and more important, if agents insist on selling it—then it is only reasonable that they be required to disclose the true rates of interest. That would permit comparison shopping, or at least give buyers some idea of what they are buying.

In 1976, the National Association of Insurance Commissioners—the organization of state regulators—prepared a model disclosure code: But it is inadequate, providing no means to compare the interest return on individual policies or the return on whole life with other investments. The Federal Trade Commission thus argues for major changes.

The FTC's whole life recommendations carry no legal weight; the McCarran-Ferguson Act delegates all insurance regulation to the states. But Americans spent $34 billion on life insurance in 1977. The market is so large and the inequities are so great that cost disclosure is imperative. If the states won't protect the consumer, there will be a strong case for Congress to do it for them.

However, President Carter endorsed the FTC staff-report disclosure recommendations in a letter circulated to the governors of all the states early in 1980, on the eve of the Senate debate on the Cannon Insurance Amendment to the Federal Trade Commission Act. The amendment was designed to keep the FTC's hands out of the insurance business.

The president wrote, "The [FTC] model regulation is designed to provide meaningful disclosure of life insurance costs. . . . This is an important initiative the states can take to promote price competition and assure that the life insurance market is responsive to the needs of consumers."

The *Journal of Commerce* in New York called the president's letter to the governors "an end run around the Senate Commerce Committee's effort to tie the FTC's hands."

The life companies, meanwhile, began lining up support of property and casualty insurors in support of their drive to curb the FTC and prevent a tough federally inspired disclosure program. They met with some success. Andre Maisonpierre, a vice-president of the Alliance of American Insurors, a property-casualty trade association, backed the life companies' position.

Even before the FTC staff began the study that led to the bombshell report in mid-1979, there was increasing clamor for federal oversight of state regulation and even for repeal of the McCarran-Ferguson Act and for turning the regulation of the industry over to Washington.

These demands came up, somewhat obliquely, in 1973 and 1974, during hearings on the stifling of information about

the life companies' financial practices and treatment of policyholders, before the Senate Subcommittee on Antitrust and
Monopoly, headed by Senator Philip A. Hart.

Ralph Nader, the kingpin of consumerist crusaders,
Herbert Denenberg, the former Pennsylvania Insurance Commissioner, Professor Joseph M. Belth, of Indiana University,
a gadfly to the life companies for many years, and many other
critics testified. What he learned from the hearings led Senator Hart to introduce the Truth in Life Insurance Bill drafted
by Dean Sharp, the subcommittee counselor. But after the
untimely death of Senator Hart this bill languished. The
committee now is headed by Senator Howard Metzenbaum,
who has shown considerable investigative and crusading zeal,
most recently in investigating abuses of credit life insurance.

But is disclosure enough, or will a federal standard result in the same kind of fiasco that efforts to achieve adequate
and effective state disclosure standards have been, according
to the *New York Times* editorial?

I think that the FTC staff report is on target in most of
its criticisms of the insurance companies that dominate the
industry, and I doubt seriously whether disclosure will be
enough to bring on real and just reform. At least, it will not
be enough for the federal government to require disclosure
of the true costs and true yields of the different kinds of
policies. Such a disclosure rule could not work miracles,
simply because the business is too complicated and too filled
with opportunities for greed.

It is also necessary to open completely the books and
records of the mutual-life-insurance companies. These giants
are run by self-perpetuating managements. Opening the win-
dows and making their books freely available would disclose
many things that might make the 1979 FTC staff report pretty

tame reading by comparison. We would learn the details of much gross waste, poor management, and extravagant salaries and bonuses. In many cases, irregular and outright illegal activities and plain examples of corporate crime would be uncovered.

In May 1980, the FTC suffered a defeat in its efforts to bring about insurance-industry reform when Senate and House conferees put severe limits on its continuing ability to conduct investigations of the industry. The commission can conduct new inquiries only if requested to do so by a majority vote of either the House or Senate Commerce Committees, and such authorization will expire at the end of the Congress in which it is given. The conferees also reaffirmed that the McCarran-Ferguson Act is the basis of national insurance policy and said that if the FTC wants the McCarran-Ferguson Act changed, it should ask Congress to change it instead of trying to bring about change by investigations of its own.

It would be too much to say that any ground swell for repeal of the McCarran-Ferguson Act yet is evident, but more and more independent insurance agents and more academic economists are asking why the life-insurance companies, since they do sell their products as investments, should not be under the same antitrust regulations as everyone else.

Probably the most unfortunate thing about the FTC staff report is its length. It is so cumbersome that the general press and broadcasters still may not have presented completely accurate digests of it.

David C. Fix, an FTC lawyer, stood up like Daniel in the lions' den before a meeting of the National Association of Life Underwriters in Detroit late in 1979 and implied that the press was responsible for the widespread impression that the FTC staff was hopelessly biased in favor of term insur-

ance and against whole-life insurance and was in fact preju-
diced against the industry. But although he said that the FTC
staff people were completely objective and interested only in
making the observable facts public, Fix did not back down on
any of the recommendations of the report.

What are the main things the FTC report urged, aside
from publishing its own comparative estimates of the costs
of different life-insurance policies and the yields consumers
can hope to realize from them? The best highlights of the report have appeared in the insurance trade press. In this day of
expensive newsprint, the FTC report had little chance of
competing for big space in the press or for time on the air
with such stirring things as the aftermath of the Three Mile
Island accident and events in Iran.

One of the important recommendations was that agents
be required to furnish applicants for life insurance or annuities complete projections of the interest and dividend
yields and calculations of the net cost over the life of the
policy *before* the prospective buyer signs the application or
gives the agent a check. By contrast, the model disclosure
code of the National Association of Insurance Commissioners
requires these disclosures to be made only when the policy is
delivered.

Another recommendation of the report would give the
policy buyer ten days in which to change his or her mind,
return the policy, and demand a refund. Another would require agents in those states whose insurance departments issue
consumers' guides to buying life insurance to furnish every
prospective policy buyer with a copy of the guide.

But the controversial and the most complex of the
recommendations concerned the type of indices to be used in
helping consumers compare the relative merits of different

policies in the same company and the policies offered by different companies.

The FTC staff wants a single index figure used. It reports some companies now give prospective buyers as many as six different indices and that the so-called yardsticks are confusing and often contradictory. But it appeared that the FTC staff had little real hope of finding a satisfactory single index. Therefore, it urged the use of the Linton yield index, invented by actuary Albert M. Linton, which the FTC people like very much, as a companion to the surrender-unit-cost measurement favored by the National Association of Insurance Commissioners. The Linton yield index shows the annual rate of return on the cash-value portion of a whole-life insurance policy. A policy with a ten-year Linton yield index of 3.5 will earn 3.5 percent compound interest yearly on the savings portion of the policy if premiums are paid for ten years. The higher the Linton yield, the more attractive the policy.

But the Linton index doesn't measure many factors about a whole-life insurance policy and the company that writes it. Neither does the surrender cost, for that matter. Nevertheless, some insurance companies are starting to quote Linton yields on their policies, and some of the consumer magazines are starting to use them in articles about the cost of insurance.

The surrender-unit cost is expressed as the dollar cost per thousand dollars of life insurance in force, based on cash surrender at varying periods. The lower the surrender-unit cost, the more attractive the policy is considered to be. But critics of this measurement say that it is even more meaningless by itself than the Linton yield index. It is used by *Consumer Reports* magazine.

The FTC staff report had some other conclusions that drew almost apoplectic reactions from life-insurance bigshots. It said the nonparticipating cash-value whole-life policies of stock life companies were "low yield fixed value saving mediums uniquely unsuited to coping with accelerated inflation."

It pointed out that neither dividend-paying nor nonparticipating cash-value whole-life policies earn a penny for their purchasers in their early years. Both have big negative cash values in these years to pay the big selling costs, including hefty agents' commissions. And over the first twenty years of both kinds of policies, the FTC said, the yields were "extraordinarily low." At twenty years, the average yield for the dividend-paying policies was 3.71 percent and that for non-participating policies 2.4 percent. Compared with what a savings bank or some financial institution will pay you on your money these days, that's worse than peanuts. There are even insurance companies issuing tax-deferred annuities at interest rates of 12.25 percent these days.*

However, the establishment life companies and their trade associations of agents rushed into the fray to say that the FTC people were just plain lying, that the average yield on whole-life cash-value policies is nearer 5.5 percent than 1.3 percent. They accused the FTC staff people of ignoring the value of the policies' fringe benefits and making unfair investment analyses similar to comparing apples with oranges. They also accused the FTC people of underestimating legitimate life-insurance-company expenses.

The report found some utterly astonishing variations in the yields on the same type of policy issued by different

* See chapter 12.

companies. It found one company paying only 1.52 percent on a twenty-five-thousand dollar policy issued to a thirty-five-year-old person while another company was paying 7.61 percent on an almost identical policy. Yet this information, which the FTC managed to uncover, is not available to the public and presumably not freely available to independent agents—so how are you going to go out and buy the policy that pays 7.61 percent? The implication is that it's some sort of "sweetheart deal."

In one of his speeches attacking the FTC staff report, Armand Stalnaker, the chairman of the Council of Life Insurance, said that he also believed the report to be a challenge and an opportunity to the industry "to reexamine our business." To that I say, "Amen!"

He went on to say that from now on, life insurance cannot be a strictly commercial business but must become a quasi-public institution. Accordingly, he said, the companies "must perform their functions on a high plane, certainly on a plane that is substantially above what is expected generally in the marketplace."

He also warned that future criticism of the industry "will not be as clumsy or as ill-informed as that of the FTC staff report." I hope you find that this book fits that prophecy.

Let's look a minute at the implications of Stalnaker's remarks. What exactly is a quasi-public institution? A stockholder-owned electric utility comes instantly to mind. Does Stalnaker want life-insurance companies to be regulated the way electric utilities are? The states rigorously set the return on investment an electric utility is permitted to earn, and if it earns more than that by miscalculation, it is required to make refunds to its customers.

Electric utilities cannot raise or lower rates a penny

without the consent of the regulators. Their accounting procedures are rigorously prescribed by the regulators. Their salaries and expense budgeting are subject to regulatory control. The state regulators can disallow expenditures they deem excessive in setting the company's rate base on which its charges to consumers are set. In the last few years, as inflation has so cruelly eroded everyone's paycheck, the utilities and management consultants and executive recruiters who serve utility companies have been complaining that the states don't allow them a sufficient profit margin to pay competitive executive salaries. Therefore, they say, they are able to recruit only mediocre talent, and this leads to relatively inefficient management. This propaganda is somewhat overdone; most utilities are fairly well managed.

But the fact that Mr. Stalnaker is reduced to thinking of life-insurance companies as "quasi-public institutions" is most revealing.

3. *Failures of State Regulation*

STATE REGULATION of life insurance as we know it today is largely the creation of two popular heroes of American political history.

One was a scholarly, determined, energetic man, an easterner of great personal charm and high intellect who went to bed on a November night in 1916 thinking he had been elected president of the United States, only to find out at breakfast that in the waning hours of the night California had swung the election, to keep Woodrow Wilson in the White House.

The other was a swashbuckling western rancher and mining lawyer, a rugged individualist who was loved by thousands but so authoritarian in many of his ideas that he was called a fascist. He was a frank imperialist and a military jingoist whose influence on Dwight Eisenhower and John Foster Dulles played no small part in ultimately getting us bogged down in the misguided and ill-fated war in Vietnam.

The first hero, of course, was Charles Evans Hughes. As a crusading young lawyer-politician, he conducted the famous investigation of the life-insurance companies by the New York legislature early in this century. State regulation already had failed the public dismally once. It was so benign and inept that companies went broke regularly, often fraudulently, and failed to pay death claims. Policies were frequently so deceitfully written that vaudeville comics made them a constant target of their acid wit. They cracked such jokes as the one about the widow who learned that the only way she could have collected insurance on her husband was if he had been killed by a falling star exactly at high noon on the twenty-ninth day of February.

Miraculously, Hughes cleaned up the whole mess in a single year. He got the New York legislature to adopt new life-insurance laws and set up a model life-insurance regulatory system that was copied swiftly by all the other states. It ended all the worst abuses that were perceived at the time. It made Hughes a famous man, and even though he missed the White House he became chief justice of the United States Supreme Court and was universally admired.

But the regulatory system Hughes created didn't have to cope with serious inflation until long after World War II. It did have to cope with the Great Depression though, and it failed the test. Between the stock market crash in October 1929 and President Franklin Roosevelt's inauguration in 1933, so many businesses failed and so many people lost their jobs that the life-insurance companies were flooded with demands for policy loans and with requests from people wanting to cash in their cash value policies. The companies panicked.

Just before FDR's inauguration a secret meeting of ex-

ecutives of the big eastern establishment life companies and
a score of state insurance commissioners was held in New
York. At this meeting the companies tossed a bombshell on
the floor: They proposed a moratorium on issuing policy loans
and on honoring cash-value-surrender demands.

Since the companies and their agents had sold the policies largely by proclaiming that insured persons had an abso-
lute right to borrow on their policies or cash them in, these
state commissioners at first said that the moratorium proposal
was grossly immoral and clearly illegal.

But these days before FDR took office, after the final
collapse of the Hoover administration's economic policies
had caused a total shutdown of the banks, the state insurance
commissioners caved in, and the moratorium went into effect.

State regulation had failed the people a second time.
The house that Hughes built had fallen down.

Starting in 1941, with the creation of the New York
State Guarantors Corporation, steps were taken to prevent
another such catastrophe. This guarantors corporation was so
structured that if any life-insurance company domiciled in
New York got in financial difficulty, all the other companies
in the state would have to cooperate to rescue it. Many other
states now have created such protective devices for their
policyholders.

By the end of World War II some people were becoming
concerned about another aspect of life-insurance regulation.
The business had become increasingly concentrated in the big
mutual firms and the larger multi-line stock companies that
operated all over the country, or at least in many states.
Clearly, these companies were engaged in interstate commerce, both in selling insurance and in their vast investment
activity in securities and real estate. So a movement devel-

oped aimed at bringing them under federal regulation like
the railroads, airlines, trucking lines, and the interstate
securities-trading-and-investment industry.

The establishment companies did not like this idea.
They had found it fairly easy to handle the state insurance
departments by following the timehonored strategy of divide
and conquer, but unified federal regulation would be a much
more formidable police giant. Moreover, the White House
could certainly be depended on to take a strong consumerist
stand about life insurance if it was brought under federal
regulation, and issues arising from it could be debated in
national election campaigns.

Therefore, toward the end of the war, the companies
put up a tremendous lobbying effort to preserve state regulation. They found an able champion and hero in Senator Pat
McCarran of Nevada.

McCarran was the kind of man most people liked even
if they hated his principles and denounced him roundly in
public. He got the McCarran-Ferguson Act passed. Its guts
are contained in a single short sentence: "No act of Congress
shall be construed to invalidate, impair or supersede any law
enacted by any state for the purpose of regulating insurance."
This applies so long as the states do it effectively.

This means, of course, that any act of Congress to estab-
lish even a minor regulation or reform of the insurance business must first repeal the McCarran-Ferguson Act or else
leave the real business of enforcement up to the states. All
this was discussed at great length during the debate over
whether Congress should set minimum standards for the states
on no-fault automobile insurance.

The McCarran-Ferguson Act has also been an effective

barrier against the maintaining of class-action lawsuits that policyholders have brought against life-insurance companies in the federal courts. Such a suit filed against four big mutual companies in 1972, alleging price-fixing, dubious accounting, cozy executive benefits, squandering of money on noninsurance ventures, and undemocratic self-perpetuation of management by failing to give the policyholders real voting power, was dismissed by a federal judge on the ground that the McCarran-Ferguson Act deprived the federal courts of jurisdiction.

Vociferous critics of state regulation, and their numbers are growing, insist that although many of the state commissioners are undeniably well meaning and capable, they are as a group rather easily manipulated and intimidated by the life-insurance establishment. The publicized activities of the National Association of Insurance Commissioners do little to contradict this charge. Most of the NAIC's programs are timid and unimaginative. So are the activities of the Conference of Insurance Legislators, which purports to be a band of shining knights in armor, members of legislatures dedicated to defending the rights of policyholders. The conference actually seems to act much more like a transmission belt or a front organization for the industry establishment.

A few years back, the NAIC put out a model state consumers' shopping guide to life insurance. It contains a vast amount of useful information, but critics claim it is biased in favor of whole-life cash-value insurance, as against term life, and seeks to gloss over some of the worst failings of life insurance.

One more big failure on the part of state insurance commissioners to put the interests of policyholders ahead of the privileges of the companies could bring on federal regulation and cause virtually all the state officials to be superseded and lose their jobs.

Two glaring failures of state regulation will become apparent when I discuss double dipping in credit life insurance (chapter 6) and scare selling in cancer insurance (chapter 5). Only three states have banned cancer insurance, and none of the state regulators has done anything to stop the enormous ripoff of the public by both insurance companies and banks and finance companies through overcharges on credit life insurance.

Another big problem with state regulation is that it is impossible to insulate it sufficiently from politics. After all, the regulators are political appointees and must depend on members of the state legislatures for moral support and for the funds to operate their departments. All politicians and bureaucrats are vulnerable in some degree to pressures from people who have axes to grind and therefore make political contributions in order to influence legislative and departmental policy. The life-insurance business has long maintained powerful lobbies in all the state capitals for this purpose. Moreover, the state regulators are dependent to a considerable extent on the companies for technical and financial information on which to base their decisions.

On the other hand, their own self-esteem and concern for their status forbids the regulators to be servile toward the insurance companies. They must prevent outright defaults on policies and bankruptcy scandals and must assist in prosecutions of insurance people for embezzlement, fraudulent accounting, violations of the securities laws, and other criminal acts.

It boils down to the fact that state regulation costs the

taxpayers a tidy sum, and there is an increasing feeling that the public does not get enough benefits from it.

The sixty-four-dollar question is, How can federal intervention improve this situation? Probably in two ways. The federal government is vastly bigger and more powerful than any state. People who scarcely know what city is the capital of their home state listen when a Washington bureaucrat speaks. People who won't go to the trouble to vote for governor do not fail to vote in presidential elections.

But the federal bureaucrat also is more vulnerable to public opinion than the state official. A federal agency is a shining target for the Ralph Naders and other crusaders, who would often be reduced to thumb-sucking despair if they could take their causes only to the fifty separate state legislatures and a multitude of offices filled with state bureaucrats.

4. *The Confession*

I N SPITE OF THEIR bitter criticism of the FTC staff report's conclusions, it is plain fact that the leaders of the life-insurance establishment admitted the truth of virtually all the report's charges five years before they were made.

This confession was not intentional, nor was it made available to the public or even to the army of life-insurance companies' employees and agents. Nevertheless, enough copies of this tacit confession were printed for private perusal by the industry's top executives so that eventually several thousand photocopies were made of the twenty-six-page document, and many people learned of its contents. Undoubtedly the FTC staff obtained copies of it. So did many, if not all, state insurance commissioners, although nothing happened to indicate that the 1974 *Trend Report* of the Institute of Life Insurance (called the American Council of Life Insurance since it moved from New York to Washington, which is a

more convenient place for lobbying) made much impression
on the state regulatory officials.

The institute had been in the habit of publishing periodic
trend reports for some time, but the 1974 document was a
real blockbuster. It was based on abstracts provided by more
than a hundred top company executives, and it made the chill-
ing declaration that the four industry leaders chosen to write
the final draft had concluded that, in the present inflationary
climate, the industry was "on a self-destruct course" if it
continued its "present emphasis on individual whole life
products."

The four persons who reached this conclusion were
Kenneth M. Wright, chief economist of the American Life
Insurance Associations, Mona G. Coogan, manager of busi-
ness economics for the Metropolitan Life Insurance Com-
pany; J. Robert Ferrari, chief economist of the Prudential
Insurance Company of America, and Francis H. Schott, vice-
president and economist of the Equitable Life Assurance
Society of the United States.

Like many confidential corporate forecasts intended for
top executives, this 1974 life insurance *Trend Report* attempted to predict various future prospects based on alterna-
tive possibilities. The possibilities were labeled Scenarios 1,
2, and 3. Scenario 1—continued high inflation at rates exceeding ten percent a year—is what eventually happened, so
that's the one we'll deal with mainly in this chapter.

Scenario 2 hoped for a leveling off of inflation to an
annual rate of 4.5 percent, with no new wars or such nasty
events as the cutoff of Iranian oil has proved to be. Scenario
3 also envisioned a big drop in inflation, after a rise to about
twelve percent by 1977, resulting in local wars around the
world and a wave of strikes and other disturbances so large

that it would be followed by an authoritarian reaction, a crackdown in the United States in 1978 that would be, according to one's personal interpretation, either a fascist coup (the *Trend Report* used no labels, however) or a healthy return to law and order and sensible economics coupled with a "rigorous fiscal policy"—a phrase that means high taxes for the masses and very low taxes for the wealthy and powerful.

The four who wrote the *Trend Report* obviously felt that Scenario 1 was what we were going to get, and they were dead right. Also, they found all three scenarios equally unpleasant. Under Scenario 3, for example, they didn't think a dictator or just a government committed to "centralization of economic management" would have much sympathy or time for the life-insurance business. They said such a regime likely "would largely destroy the opportunity of individuals to fund their own personalized security programs"—that is, the opportunity for life-insurance companies to sell cash-value policies or even such straight investment instruments as annuities.

In addition to the remark about being on a self-destruct course, the "general comments" starting on page 8 of the *Trend Report* were enough to make the average life-insurance agent's hair stand up straight and to make policyholders reach for the telephone to call their agents and cancel much of their insurance. So the report was kept carefully out of the hands of the public and the rank-and-file agents.

But one of the comments would have pleased a lot of agents. The report said that the first two scenarios "foretell such expansion of the indexed benefits of Social Security that the large middle market would be swallowed by government benefits." Even before the *Trend Report* a number of insurance agents had complained bitterly that Social Security is unfair competition with their business, particularly since Social Security is not really insurance—it is financed to a substantial degree out of general tax revenues, in addition to payroll deduction and employer contributions.

The other harsh forecasts in these general comments were:

1. "The means to pay premiums for individual [whole-life cash-value] contracts would disappear in tax expansion."
2. "The business might seek such options as floating or in dexed rates for policy loans or even a release from the obligation of guaranteed cash values."
3. "The purchasing power of permanent life insurance will be impaired."
4. "Conditions suggest the likelihood of a major shift away from traditional cash value, whole life insurance with its fixed dollar saving element toward various forms of term insurance."
5. "Term insurance may have to be higher priced to provide the agent with compensation lost as the result of diminished whole life sales."
6. "The conditions would be good for a greater reliance on group term insurance and, particularly among the masses, on Social Security."
7. "There could be a massive drain on individual life insurance reserves and the underlying investments."
8. "Mutual companies [and stock companies selling dividend paying policies] might review dividend policy. This could include a look at the investment year method, the possibility of a level rather than an increasing dividend flow, and possible reduction of terminal dividends to recognize the market

value loss due to withdrawal of funds when asset values are depressed on a current yield basis."

Of course, the most immediately important of these conclusions is number four, which admits that people are finding that moderately priced term insurance providing adequate death benefits is far more valuable than costly whole-life cash-value policies, which often accomplish little except to earn fat commissions for agents and big profits for the life companies. It gives the lie to practically everything the companies have preached for more than a century.

If some of the forecasts of the *Trend Reports* are realized, such as number two and number eight, the entire structure of the mammoth life-insurance industry will be changed forever. I predict that such moves would almost mean further encroachment on the part of government, through amendments to the Social Security law, that would make new sales of life insurance impossible.

The remark about using the investment-year method for calculating policy dividends actually means cheating older policyholders so more attractive dividends can be offered to new policy buyers. James F. Reiskytl, associate actuary of Northwestern Mutual Life Insurance Company, charged early in 1979, in a letter to the National Association of Insurance Commissioners, that the investment-year method of fixing dividends amounted to illegal manipulation of dividends in order "to beat out competition."

In using the investment-year method, the company calculates policy dividend-payment rates on present yields of investments instead of the cumulative average yields. Thus, they do not include interest on investments made some years

back, at much lower interest rates. Therefore, in a period of
higher rates, the dividends offered new policyholders can be
made to look more attractive than they should, and this is
done at the expense of existing policyholders.

Changing Times magazine said that one of the biggest
mutual companies already has adopted the investment-year
method of calculating dividends and that an official of the
company could see nothing wrong with doing it that way.

Other important conclusions concerned what the 1974
Trend Report authors considered to be the outlook for new
life-insurance products. After reiterating the view that term
insurance would increasingly replace whole-life cash-value
policies, they said group term life insurance would become
increasingly important because "it is an indexed product to
the extent that it is related to the employee's salary."

The report pointed out that there are numerous objec-
tions to indexing as a means of dealing with inflation. (The
most important objection is that it can lull people into thinking the inflation is being coped with) but added, "If our
psychology is to be indexed then, of course, indexed life
insurance must play an important role."

Like whole life, group life insurance also has its inequi-
ties, even though it is relatively cheap and most times is paid
for entirely by the employer. A friend of mine who is still
employed at his maximum salary had his group-life coverage
cut in half three years ago because of his age. It doesn't seem
fair.

The report also concluded that companies will sell a
wider range of policies because "without a wide range of
products it will be very difficult for an agent to survive
financially." On this subject, the *Trend Report* indulged in a

frankness the authors would hardly have liked to submit to public gaze. It said, "While this does not relate to the type of life insurance product likely to be sold, it does speak to the product mix the life insurance agent is likely to have in his portfolio. And, therefore, it speaks to the amount of time, training and expertise the agent may need for selling and servicing the life products of the future."

Sounds nice, but what does it really mean? The more you look at it, the more it seems as if life insurance is getting ready to substitute packaging and marketing for full measure and worth of products. It reminds one of. a film called *The Hucksters,* which starred Clark Gable, Deborah Kerr, and Sidney Greenstreet. Greenstreet played the president of the Beautee Soap Company, a role obviously patterned on the career of George Washington Hill, the advertising genius of American Tobacco Company. He tells Gable in the film, "There isn't any damn difference in soap except a little perfumery. All the rest is advertising and selling. We outadvertise and outsell our competitors; that's all there is to it."

After showing their distaste for policies indexed to cope with inflation, the *Trend Reports* authors next deal with proposals for automatic increases in coverage but add, "We recognize that the agent frequently objects to automatic increases in coverage, but we wonder if that psychology can be permitted to predominate in the future."

The FTC staff report made crystal clear that many agents object to automatically increased coverage because it deprives them of the opportunity to write a new policy with a fat initial premium that they can now write when dear Doctor Rostomy's practice is doing so well that he decides he needs more life insurance. The inference of the *Trend Report* re-

mark on automatic coverage also is crystal clear: If automatic coverage increases turn out well for the companies, the
agents can swallow it or get lost.

I can only say that in this area, I disagree not only with
the FTC staff report, but with the *Trend Report* as well.
Instead of preventing agents from earning a rightful liveli-
hood after creating present and future business for an insurance company, I would prefer that commissions be paid on
automatic increases in coverage and the money be obtained
by eliminating waste in the home offices of the companies.

As a matter of fact, some articles in the insurance trade
press and the general press have recently suggested that the
general agency system may have to be abandoned. And the
Trend Report predicts considerable difficulty in recruiting
young persons to go into the life-insurance business in the
coming years because "inflation will abort thrift as an achievable goal in the minds of the public, and this will render
undesirable a sales career in exclusively life sales."

This condition has existed for the thirty-six years I have
been around the industry, but it took till 1974 for others to
wake up to this fact. If insurance people are doing a professional job, they must know and sell all lines of insurance and
even other money products.

We can wonder whether young people being interviewed
for life-insurance sales jobs are being told this.

The report also said that the cost of recruiting agents
has skyrocketed and the industry's old problem of a high
turnover of young salespeople is not getting any better. College employment offices will tell you quite bluntly that when
the on-campus recruiting season comes each year, insurance
companies are reduced to taking the leavings, the graduates
whose average grades weren't high enough to win them good

offers from companies in the fields for which they trained. So you find a lot of people with engineering and other professional degrees among young life-insurance salespersons. You also find a lot of people who trained to be teachers but couldn't find jobs in that overcrowded field.

The *Trend Report* also forecast the death of a lot of small and medium-sized life companies. That hardly surprises anyone who watches the stock market even casually. Very few life stocks have done very well since their prices peaked out in 1964–65.

The report also forecast a possible "detrimental effect on the persistency rate of our business." That's a fancy way of saying that more people will stop paying on their policies.

And a cutback was forecast in lavish and ostentatious offices for life-company executives. Drastic changes in employee compensation were predicted. The concluding pages dwelt heavily on one theme—that the industry would have to get rid of a lot of humble and marginal workers and make promotion faster for good employees. (One major company shocked its employees with top-to-bottom layoffs in 1978.)

Another admission in the report was that companies that are already selling wide portfolios of term insurance "appear to be in a better position to weather the inflationary storms" than the companies still concentrating on whole life.

That also seems to put the lie to a vast amount of the propaganda the establishment companies have preached as gospel for a hundred and twenty-five years.

But perhaps the most revealing statement in the whole study is at the bottom of page 22: "Top executives, not so mobile as the technical group, might suffer the most and, therefore innovative bonus systems might be in order."

5. *Typical Abuses*

MORE THAN A CENTURY AGO, Phineas T. Barnum remarked of suckers, "There's one born every minute."

However, the astute showman actually had an affectionate regard for suckers. He believed in giving them a pretty fair shake for their money. His circus, menagerie, concerts, and other attractions always were first rate, even though the ballyhoo by which he sold tickets and gained worldwide publicity was composed of elaborate and barefaced hokum. He also knew that the customers were amused by the ballyhoo.

There always have been people in the world, though, quite as aware as Barnum of the ever-renewable supply of suckers but totally lacking Barnum's conscience. They operate on the principle that the easiest and most profitable way to do business is to rip the suckers off mercilessly, not just by using deceitful advertising and ballyhoo to make sales, but by delivering a shoddy product, a product that is grossly overpriced or isn't really needed.

The life-insurance business has had more than its share of these gross abuses. The endowment policy was one such abuse. We will see later that the heavily front-end-loaded annuity is another. Cancer insurance, a current fad, is also such an abuse.

Still another abuse is the mail-order sale of so called budget-priced term insurance at prices that turn out to be at least twice those of other comparable term insurance. I am not attacking all mail-order marketers of life insurance. Doubtless, most mail-order policies are quite fairly priced, considering that frequently no medical examination is required to buy them. But some are quite plainly abuses. Unfortunately, some of the mail-order policies that are the poorest values are offered by life-insurance subsidiaries of conglomerates.

Many insurance companies—life, property and casualty, and even multiline enterprises—have been acquired in recent years by industrial and commercial conglomerates. Some conglomerates have even established new insurance companies to take advantage of special opportunities related to their other enterprises; these include health insurance, credit life insurance, or automobile-maintenance insurance extending coverage some years beyond the manufacturers' warranties.

These invasions of the insurance field by noninsurance corporations have raised questions. In the frenzied merger activity in the United States in the past twenty years, the business world has seen plenty of prosperous businesses destroyed by mergers, either by looting, cynical liquidation to reduce competition or by the inability of the acquiring company to give the purchased business as good management as it enjoyed under its original owners. That could happen to some insurance companies gobbled up by conglomerates.

A lot of these unfortunate occurrences are the direct consequence of the "bottom line" management philosophy so religiously taught in our graduate business schools. Candidates for the degree of master of business administration are taught that their careers will depend on how regularly they can show an increase for the departments or subsidiaries they are given to run on the "bottom line"—yield on invested capital or as a percentage of sales, according to the nature of the business. This can lead to cynical management abuses.

A popular magazine recently described one of the most fascinating examples of a conglomerate making big profits out of life insurance. The activities of the mail-order life insurance subsidiary of a well-known manufacturer were the subject. The article charged that by means of vast amounts of very deceptive television advertising, followed up by mailed brochures, the company is selling naïve families "budget-priced twenty-year term insurance" policies with face values of ten thousand or twenty thousand dollars that actually cost two to two and a half times as much as other term insurance. The article said the firm advertised that its minimum policy cost was only sixteen cents a day, which seems cheap until you discover there are companies with good ratings willing to sell the same policies for eight cents a day.

The author said that profits on the business are obviously enormous, even though television advertising is quite expensive, and the profit will be increased in time because a high proportion of the policy buyers will not keep on paying for the insurance but will let it lapse and the company will never have to pay the death benefits.

What this firm is doing, the article said, is essentially selling term life insurance without any cash values at the same high prices and with the same low protection levels as some whole-life policies.

The insurance is in level premium with level death benefits, sold without medical examination, but it is restricted to persons between the ages of eighteen and forty-five. The older you are when you buy it, the higher the premium. If you buy it at age twenty (for males), the level annual premium for the next twenty years for a ten thousand dollar death benefit is $50.80. At age thirty it's $66.48, and at age forty, it's $118.32. Premiums for women are somewhat less because of their longer average lifespan.

Let's emphasize that unlike the more commonly sold term insurance, these policies have neither a diminishing death benefit nor a rising annual premium.

The magazine contrasted the ten-thousand-dollar policies sold at various ages with similar policies offered by several other life-insurance companies and by mutual savings banks in Massachusetts and New York. One of the more moderately priced life companies offered a ten-thousand-dollar twenty-year level-death-benefit term policy at age twenty for a premium that starts at $19.92 a year and rises to $25.52 at age thirty-nine. Over the full term the buyer would pay $467.60 for this death protection as against $1,067.10 for the conglomerate policy.

The big point is that insurance such as the conglomerate is selling—and they had sold $400 million worth through mid-1979—is part and parcel of the high-profit emphasis of the packaging-and-marketing psychology of "bottom-line economics." It is what makes so much of American business operate on the ripoff principle, and it is probably responsible in no small degree for the decline in our national productivity and our failing competitive position in international markets. The aim of this philosophy is to get an ever-bigger yield out of every dollar of sales any way you can, and never mind the consumers: "They are born suckers, and if we don't take them somebody else will."

Naturally, runaway inflation increases business cynicism and makes businessmen justify in their own eyes this kind of rapacious marketing.

But it gyps the people who buy the policies horribly. The insurance is sold by following Joseph Goebbels's famous maxim that the bigger a lie is and the more often and the more loudly it is repeated, the easier it is to get people to believe it—and buy.

A young couple in their twenties or thirties does not need a paltry ten thousand or even twenty thousand dollars in death protection today. They need thirty thousand to one hundred thousand dollars, according to what they can afford.

The big trouble, as we have pointed out earlier, is that life-insurance pricing is downright chaotic. However, if it were only the complex age tables and the equally complex tables on face amounts and special benefits, then any reasonably well-educated agent with a hand calculator could figure out the answers to the really important questions pretty quickly.

But the agent will flounder on company-to-company comparisons, with their baffling and often totally illogical contradictions. Only the very experienced agent can find his or her way through this jungle with reasonable promptness. The captive agent, of course, is forbidden even to make the effort. The establishment life-insurance companies have created a climate in which people literally have no idea what the price of life insurance ought to be. The companies have fostered this public ignorance and exploited it for generations to make high profits.

The managements of some of the conglomerates that have pushed into the life-insurance business undoubtedly see in this widespread public ignorance a golden opportunity to make big killings in the next few years. In what other line of business are the customers so ill-informed about the product's actual worth, so like sheep ready for the shearing?

Everyone knows how to compare the values of things sold in stores; and although you can sell a really fancy automobile for a big price on glamour, no one's going to pay Cadillac prices for compact cars. But that's precisely what some of the "bottom line" insurance-company managers are selling—and they're getting away with it.

From time to time, though, a life-insurance fad comes along with its sales appeal based largely on scare selling— arousing unjustified fear among prospective customers and using that fear to reap high profits while providing inferior insurance benefits. We are being subjected to such a fad now—it is called cancer insurance. Fifteen million Americans have bought it, paying annual premiums estimated to average just under a hundred and fifty dollars for family policies with a face value of two hundred thousand dollars. All but two million of these families have bought their policies within the past five years, although cancer insurance has been on the market for at least twenty years. The past five years are the period in which an average of two to four new cancer scares have arisen every week.

Cancer insurance is not exactly a gigantic deal. The total amount of premium income it brings in probably is not much more than five hundred million dollars a year.

Not many life companies write cancer insurance. At least three states have outlawed the business, and half a dozen others have cracked down hard on the advertising and sales techniques of the companies that do sell it.

Changing Times magazine denounced cancer insurance as "a bad buy" in its December 1979 issue. In Congress, the House Select Committee on Aging has been investigating the business. The federal General Accounting Office reported that the loss ratio of the companies that sell it—that is, the proportion of premium income that they actually paid out in claims —ranged downward from fifty-five percent to an astounding nineteen percent for one company. Even fifty-five percent is a very low loss ratio for any life-insurance or health-insurance operation. By contrast Blue Cross-Blue Shield pays out in claims ninety cents of every dollar it takes in, but of course, Blue Cross-Blue Shield is a nonprofit operation. Nevertheless, it makes enough money to pay very good salaries on that high loss ratio.

The handful of companies that sell cancer insurance are big advertisers, using direct mail, periodicals, and radio and television to carry the sales messages. At least three of the companies have been accused by public officials or agencies of deceptive advertising and unfair sales practices.

The main complaints against the companies selling cancer insurance are:

• In spite of the big face values of the policies, many of them do not pay any more for cancer treatment and care than conventional medical and hospitalization policies or Medicare pay for the same premium dollar.

• Massachusetts investigators said cancer insurance sold

in the state paid for only about thirty percent of the cost of a typical serious cancer case.

• The Federal Trade Commission staff said a cancer-insurance policy is like a lottery ticket "and not a very good gamble either."

• *Changing Times* said many cancer-insurance policies have major exclusion clauses denying benefits to the insured that are not readily apparent to the policy buyer and are not adequately explained.

• The policies pay only for "definitive cancer treatment" as a rule; they pay nothing for diagnosis, pathology reports, or cancer-related complications.

• Some of the policies pay for chemotherapy or radiological treatment only if the patient is hospitalized; yet current medical practice is to give most of these treatments on an outpatient basis. The policies usually pay nothing for rehabilitation, which also is done on an outpatient basis.

• The policies do not take effect until 60 to 120 days after purchase. If a malignancy is discovered during this period it may not be covered by the cancer policy.

• As stated earlier in this chapter, the companies exaggerate the prevalence of cancer in the United States grossly in their advertising, exploiting and even creating a hysterical fear of cancer.

• The companies spread the idea that a person can collect simultaneously under two or more health insurance policies, including a cancer policy, although this by no means is always true.

Although cancer insurance appears to resemble renewable-term life insurance and is sold without a medical examination, and although the premiums are relatively modest, remember that it pays no death benefit unless death is caused directly by cancer and no disability benefits except for cancer.

So the cancer-insurance business would appear to be another example of insurance huckstering, abusing the basic concept of life insurance to rip off the public by selling people protection they don't really need.

As a matter of fact, a close analysis shows that the perils that any individual faces in life are so numerous that to insure against each of these hazards would necessitate forking over your whole salary check each week to insurance companies.

6. *Double Dipping in Credit Life*

ANOTHER LIFE-INSURANCE scandal that is cheating Americans of huge sums is the gross abuse of credit life insurance.

About $179.25 billion worth of credit life insurance was in force in the United States at the end of 1979. The 1980 *Life Insurance Fact Book* says that $1.78 billion was collected in 1979 in credit-life premiums, but actual collections were much higher, an estimated $2.5 billion, because premiums are collected in advance for loans running for eighteen months to several years, but the companies report only the portions applicable to the current year. There seems to be good reason to suspect that at least one-third of the collections represent scandalous overcharges.

Unlike the abuses of whole-life cash-value insurance, credit-life chicanery is an abuse of term insurance, selling the coverage at inflated rates of from four to ten times the cost of other term life insurance. Indeed, short-term credit-life rates appear to be much higher than those of either whole-life cash-value insurance or health insurance. The excuse generally given for the high rates is that no medical examination is required and no questions are asked the insured about her or his health. But this is not entirely true. Credit life insurance is always written to guarantee payment of a loan in case of the death of the borrower, and many lending institutions ask questions about the borrower's health before making the loan. The mere fact that the loan application has been accepted is thus a guarantee to the insurance company that the borrower is reasonably healthy.

Credit life insurance is cynically claimed by its vendors to be cheap—"only a few pennies a day" to relieve your survivors of the painful necessity of paying off the loan if you die. Don't you believe it! Credit life insurance can add four hundred dollars to the cost of a five-thousand-dollar automobile financed for five years.

The particularly loathsome aspect of credit life insurance is a "double-dipping ripoff" of the insured borrowers by two sets of deceptive hucksters, the insurance companies and the banks and finance companies who serve as their vendors and who get the bigger share of the ripoff profit. They accomplish this because the premium is not paid directly by the insured, who is the borrower, but is added to the face amount of the loan and interest is charged on it at the same rate as the principal of the loan.

That's only the tip of the iceberg. What the gullible borrower who consents to having his or her loan insured by credit life insurance (it is not required by law, no matter what the bank or finance company officer may tell you) doesn't know is that banks and finance companies often deliberately purchase the most expensive credit life insurance they can find and pass the cost on to borrowers because that inflates their commissions as vendors of the insurance and gives them bigger premiums to charge high interest on.

Even though it is not required by law, the lending company can require a credit-life-insurance policy covering the loan of its own volition. But if the lender tells you it's required by law, you can sue for damages. The reason for the deception is usually to stop the loan applicant from shopping around to find cheaper insurance. There have been so many complaints recently about the abuses of credit life insurance that the Consumers Credit Life Insurance Association, composed of insurance companies that sell the stuff, recently told the Illinois State Insurance Department it now favors giving borrowers more option about whether they will buy the coverage at all and even a grace period to cancel it if they change their minds.

This chastened attitude undoubtedly stems from a wave of reports that lending institutions had failed to tell borrowers the amount their loans had been increased to pay for credit life insurance or to give them any information about the cost of the insurance. That is clearly illegal but the practice appears to be widespread. In December 1979, Senator Howard Metzenbaum asked the Justice Department to investigate for possible criminal prosecution a case in which Beneficial Finance Company failed for twelve years to inform a blind couple living in Philadelphia that they were being charged for credit life insurance on their loans. A company official then told the couple that the insurance was required, which Senator Metzenbaum said was not the case. And in a lawsuit the couple accused Beneficial of adding to their loan contract a false statement that they had consented to the purchase of the insurance. According to *The Insurance Advocate* for December 1, 1979, to forestall further legal action, Beneficial canceled the blind couple's $1,200 loan balance and paid them $2,000 cash, plus $1,750 in legal fees.

Senator Metzenbaum planned late in 1979 to introduce a bill to set minimum federal standards for the states in regulating credit life insurance. He said that the Senate Judiciary Antitrust Subcommittee had been investigating credit life insurance for twelve years, and during that time the state regulatory authorities had done almost nothing to curb the abuses.

With a few noteworthy exceptions, he said, the state officials are not protecting consumers from systematic overcharges and other abuses by credit-life-insurance companies. He said that for most consumers credit life insurance costs two to four times as much as other term insurance and sometimes much more than that.

J. Robert Hunter, deputy administrator of the Federal Insurance Administration, was quoted by Brendan Jones in the *New York Times*, May 19, 1979, as saying that credit life insurance costs up to ten times as much as other life insurance or health insurance. Hunter told Jones that all credit life insurance "is a ripoff, most people don't need the stuff."

Senator Metzenbaum said that in many states less than one third of the premiums collected on credit life insurance go to pay claims, thus giving the insurance companies—and the banks and finance companies acting as their vendors—an enormous melon to split up. It is a seller's market for the creditors—that is, for the banks and finance companies—and the senator and Hunter both said that the bizarre "reverse competition" makes it a bonanza. Metzenbaum said that this phenomenon alone demonstrates the need for effective price regulation in credit life insurance and that if the states continue their apathetic attitude, Congress will have to do something about it.

Every state except Alaska has set a ceiling on credit-life-insurance rates but Metzenbaum and other critics say that these ceilings are too high. Metzenbaum said that in forty states the ceilings are so high that they permit minimum loss ratios of less than fifty percent of premiums collected. He said they ought to be lowered until the companies are required to pay out on claims about eighty percent of what they collect in premiums. The National Association of Insurance Commissioners seems to be veering in favor of aiming at minimum loss ratios of sixty percent and a general ceiling on rates of fifty cents per hundred dollars of insured loan. At least, three major credit-life underwriters testified to that effect before Metzenbaum's committee in November 1979.

Metzenbaum said that rates based on a minimum loss ratio of fifty percent are probably costing Americans nine hundred million dollars a year more to insure their consumer loans against death than if the companies had to assume that they would pay out eighty percent of their premium collections in loss claims.

The senator also said that there is much coercive selling in credit life insurance—a strong implication that if you don't go along with the lending company's deal and buy its credit insurance, you may not get the loan.

It was also testified that the actual national average annual rate on credit life insurance was around 65.5 cents per hundred dollars of loan insured and that adoption of the NAIC's sixty-percent loss limit could cut that to around 41.7 cents.

This testimony came from James H. Hunt, director of the Massachusetts State Rating Bureau. He said that in general, credit life insurance is costing people fifty-seven percent more than what the NAIC recommends, and he criticized his fellow state officials for not moving more vigorously to follow their own association's program.

New York has one of the lowest average rates on credit life insurance in the country, about forty-four cents, but Irene Alpert of the New York State Insurance Department staff said that's still too high. She said the rate ought to be not more than forty-one cents. She was quoted to this effect by Brendan Jones in the *New York Times*.

Jones said that the interest the banks charge on credit-life-insurance premiums they advance to borrowers is a bonanza at present rates and that if interest rates should fall sharply after the big 1979 rise, the banks would continue to collect the high 1979 interest rates on a very large volume of these premium advances for some time to come.

What can the individual do about the scandalous conditions in credit life insurance? Not as much as he or she can do about other life-insurance abuses. The reason is that many credit-life-insurance transactions are small and not worth going to a lot of trouble and fuss over. The insurance companies and the lenders rely on public apathy and on the fact that the ordinary borrower is so pressed for time that she or he will submit to their deception and thievery.

But if it's a fairly hefty loan, financing a car or college tuition for example, it will pay to take the time to exercise your rights. Remember these facts:

• Credit life insurance is not required by law, no matter what a bank or finance-company official may tell you.

• The lending institution can require you to take credit life insurance as a condition of granting the loan, but it cannot require you to buy the policy it is selling. You can shop around and buy your own, and by so doing you will at least save paying interest on the premium at today's high rates.

• You can and should demand a statement of the exact cost of the credit life insurance you are offered. If it is more than about forty-five cents per hundred dollars of loan per year, it is high. But nearly all the rates you are offered are certain to be quite excessive.

• Shopping for reasonably priced credit life insurance may not be easy, but your independent life-insurance agent may be able to help you. He or she may be able to find coverage at more reasonable cost.

• In New York, Pennsylvania, and probably many other states you should be able to get useful information about buying credit life insurance more reasonably by writing or telephoning your state department of insurance.

You might also write your senator and representative in congress and your state legislators demanding that something drastic be done to curb the credit-life-insurance ripoff.

7. A Smug Industry

Eimg ARLY IN 1979, the American Council of Life Insurance held a conclave on inflation at Williamsburg, Virginia. Out of the meeting came a big elaborately printed publicity kit, replete with canned speeches and press releases, sent to all the life companies and many agency heads.

After perusing the kit, one might be pardoned for concluding that its only contribution to combating inflation was that the manuscript pages were typed on both sides of the paper. The pieces in the kit posed a lot of questions, all of which had been raised before by numerous economists, businessmen, educators, politicians, and journalists. The Council of Life Insurance turned out to be more timid than these other Jeremiahs in saying what ought to be done about inflation.

Executives of insurance companies are generally known to be timid, and very few like to act responsibly, for fear of rocking the boat. More important—are the life-insurance

companies really ready to help educate the multitudes to stem
the tide of runaway inflation and save America?

The only area on which the canned speeches were very
positive concerned the appalling impact of inflation on the
cash-value life-insurance business—company profits and
agents' commissions. The kit's silence was deafening (if reading matter can be deafening) on the really big question—
what, if anything, the life companies are willing to do to help
the millions of older and not-so-old policyholders who are
stuck with high-priced life policies whose cash values and
death benefits have been eroded in comparison with other,
more conventional savings instruments. Are the companies
willing to come clean and tell the policyholders the truth?
Are they prepared to offer older customers something better
at affordable premium prices in exchange for their depre-
ciated policies?

The answer is—silence. When the companies say anything to these older customers they urge them in shrill tones
to continue paying the sacrificial tribute to the privileged life-
insurance establishment. This attitude shows that in spite of
their pious posture of being a great benefactor of humanity,
the life-insurance companies do not constitute a public-spirited
business.

Except in medical research, where it could expect to
reap a huge return in longer life expectancy and, hence,
longer premium collections, life insurance has not been particularly generous in its contributions to the public welfare.
Nor have the companies been bold and vigorous in taking
actions and stands calculated to help society advance. Steel
barons, automobile tycoons, department-store owners, oil
billionaires, publishing magnates, and successful Wall Street-
ers seem to have been much more generous.

Herbert Denenberg, the former Pennsylvania insurance commissioner, says the life companies are apathetic about the public welfare. Denenberg wrote a newspaper column for years and conducts a radio program on general consumer issues. He said that his views about the life companies had mellowed a little in recent years because he had encountered so many more villainous attitudes toward consumers on the part of other industries. However, he still thinks the life companies are too content to sit on their hands. He said that they collect statistical information that reveals serious problems in society, but as a rule they don't follow through and try to get something done about the problems.

Denenberg was made to feel the political power of the life companies after he exposed their nefarious pricing practices while he was insurance commissioner. He resigned to run for the United States Senate, in the expectation that he could regain the commissionership if he didn't make it into the Senate, but the life companies succeeded in blocking his reappointment by exerting political pressure.

In his column in the *Philadelphia Daily News* on January 3, 1980, Denenberg said that it is surprising that the public buys as much life insurance as it does "when you consider the confusing and inept marketing methods of the industry. . . . The Public Enemy No. 1 of the life insurance industry is the life insurance industry itself."

Of course, in saying that the industry is not public spirited, I am referring to the companies. Many company general agents and many independent life-insurance agents are public spirited. They work hard in charity drives, serve on the boards of many worthwhile activity groups, and often are generous with their own financial contributions. But the companies, sitting on $432.28 billion worth of assets as of the end of 1979, obviously could do a great deal more than they have. Their ineffectual and almost totally self-serving approach to fighting inflation is typical.

What have they done about education? Offhand, I can't think of an American university or college that was founded by the benevolence of an insurance magnate, nor do I know of any large-scale scholarship programs or long-term research projects funded by life-insurance companies except those few which are calculated to increase life-insurance profits if they are successful. Even in these areas the life-company funding is likely to be small compared with what comes from government agencies and other private and commercial sources.

We have in the United States a crisis in our school systems. It is caused only partly by money shortages. Population shifts, language barriers, racial tensions, the baleful influence on kids of commercial television, the fact that too many mothers have to hold down jobs and the children are left on their own much of the day, at least after school hours —all these are more serious matters than the money shortages. But money could help alleviate some of these problems, and a rich industry like the life-insurance industry could do something. It could well afford to offer help in finding solutions. It shows no signs of doing so.

Most of my readers have learned of the terrible toll that our poor school system has taken on the literacy level of our poor citizens during the past several decades. Why hasn't this industry, so rich and supposedly so humanitarian, done something to effect a better school system throughout the country?

Slaughter on the highways is one of the worst problems in America today. The property-and-casualty-insurance industry, much of which is teamed with life-insurance business in multi-line companies, sells comprehensive automobile insurance. Property-and-casualty-insurance people have tried to do something about the carnage. But even though they have to pay death or injury claims on people killed or injured in auto accidents, the *life*-insurance companies haven't made a big or particularly intelligent effort to do much about safety. The highway-safety measures of the property-and-casualty insurors have been minuscule compared with the achievements of the police, the highway engineers, and the professional safety experts. Even the automobile companies have done more than the insurance people. They have produced cars that hold the road better and stop more quickly—although there is much dispute about the sturdiness of the modern car, which is made light in weight to conserve fuel.

The motorist often finds the talk of insurance people about highway safety confusing. Many motorists get the idea that the companies are interested in proclaiming dubious safety standards for drivers only as a means of getting higher rates and earning bigger profits. Many insurance companies have also been accused of encouraging inflation of property-liability claims arising from auto accidents, as a means both of winning higher rates and of getting a reputation for being liberal on claims because such a reputation can make it easier to sell policies.

Crime is an area in which the insurance industry has shown itself to be far from public spirited. Of late, the tremendous increase in arson has compelled the fire-insurance companies to take a more resolute stand and give the police and fire marshals more support and cooperation. But far too many cases of fairly obvious arson are settled at high payouts without a struggle, and there is too much ugly gossip about complicity of insurance people in some of these smelly

arrangements. Arsonists comprise a recognized criminal profession. A veteran fire-department officer can usually tell if a
building has been torched, no matter how well arsonists
conceal their tracks.

The losses from arson are enormous. The insurance companies and the insurance trade press talk a lot about arson,
but spreading information about firebugs seems to be as far
as they are willing to go. You don't read about many arsonists
actually going to trial, and you don't hear of many property
owners being prosecuted by insurance companies because of
suspicious fires.

Probably the most glaring and cruel example of the life
companies' lack of public spirit was the way they took part
in or countenanced the wholesale "redlining" of large areas
of our biggest cities when urban decay became acute in the
1960s. Instead of trying to stem the blight that ravaged inner-
city areas, the life companies accelerated the destruction by
refusing to provide mortgage money to real estate people and
builders who wanted to acquire the rundown properties and
modernize or replace them. They just drew lines in red ink
around huge areas on the city maps and decreed that within
these bloody boundaries they would not lend a penny.

The life companies weren't the only redliners, but they
were in the forefront of this movement that created deserts of
demolished or abandoned blocks of flats, small stores, and
small factories such as the South Bronx in New York City and
many other redlined urban areas. The few remaining buildings in these areas were gutted by fires set by vandals or
became warrens inhabited by bands of dope pushers, other
criminals, and social dropouts.

No one has been able to figure out a way to rebuild into
viable neighborhoods these urban deserts created by redlin-

ing, that smug and selfish exhibition of contempt for humanity.

The impact on society of redlining extends far beyond the immediate depopulation of big neighborhoods. Thousands of small businesses that provided jobs for unskilled workers were wiped out. Industries in the more prosperous areas of the cities found it increasingly difficult to get workers because affordable rental housing was no longer available for the workers anywhere in the city. People were compelled either to leave the cities in search of work or to congregate in a few crowded ghettos. Many just went permanently on the welfare rolls.

So businesses in the more prosperous parts of the cities began to move out of town and even to go bankrupt in substantial numbers for lack of workers and customers.

City tax revenues shrank because so many buildings were abandoned or at least torn down to reduce taxes.

The social and economic changes of the late 1950s and the 1960s started the blight, but redlining turned it into a veritable cancer, and the life companies cooperated wholeheartedly in the redlining.

It can be argued that the assets of life companies are the assets of the policyholders. If this is so, then helping to build up those urban areas would have increased the assets of the tens of millions of policyholders and improved living conditions for the general population. Unfortunately, with ostrichlike lack of courage, most insurance-company executives found it easier to get out the red pencil.

The insurance industry has long been criticized for dealing with burglars who rob jewelers and private individuals of fancy baubles with the sole idea of selling the loot back to the insurance company. No one knows just how widespread this practice is, but an insurance company can avoid paying off a two-hundred-thousand-dollar loss claim by buying the jewelry back from the burglar for perhaps sixty thousand dollars. The thief thus gets fifty percent more than the going rate of twenty cents on the dollar of appraised value that the ordinary "fence" will pay.

The insurance company thereby becomes an accessory to the burglary. The police know very well what is happening, but they can't do anything about it because everyone involved will lie under oath on the witness stand.

If maneuvered into admitting that such transactions take place, the insurance people will say that they are only acting to reduce the loss and are not more culpable than someone who offers a reward for the return of lost property with no questions asked. But the reward to the thief is enormous in these cases, and he or she is assured of escaping prosecution.

Some life-insurance companies also become involved with criminals from time to time—for example, by entering into bribery deals to land big packages of business and by making large personal loans to shady characters, loans that often are illegal and utterly uncollectible. What kind of favors the life-insurance companies can get in return for these loans varies a great deal, and the information rarely leaks out.

Never in the country's history have the life companies and their owners or top-management cliques been in the vanguard of movements for social improvement. Far from taking any role in civil rights, they cooperated until after World War II with those reactionary elements who wanted to keep black people in subjugation. They were also by and large anti-Jewish in their personnel policies and dragged their feet as long as they could on social justice for females.

They did support the Prohibition movement early in this century. They are against alcoholism because an alcoholic is usually a poor insurance risk and an uncertain payer of premiums. But the companies have given not much more than lip service to the effort to solve the great narcotics evil of today. They have not faced up to this matter in an effective way.

The life companies and the other insurance companies contend that they are leaders in social progress because they provide so much mortgage money and contribute so much capital flow for industry. But they are paid very well for this, and they avoid the riskier loans that the commercial banks make.

Leaders of the industry have been less willing on the whole than other business and professional people to stand up and be counted publicly on important controversial issues. Consequently, much of their political activity has been clandestine; and clandestine political activity has traditionally been disreputable and corrupt in all societies.

This is not a pretty picture, and it is high time that all the insurance companies began to realize that their huge financial power imposes on them the obligation of genuine social, economic, and political responsibility toward all Americans—not just to their own managements.

If the insurance companies would take a reasonable part of their self-serving efforts at maintaining their privileges and high rates and divert the energy to tacking the appalling problems of crime and narcotics addiction, they would perhaps justify their appeal for public support.

Take the matter of crime. The companies could very well send people into the schools to impress on children the terrible consequence of a tolerance of crime and the so called street-wise society. More than that, they could take the lead in demanding a much-needed reform in our creaky and dilatory court procedures, which are presently heavily overbalanced in favor of the criminal and against the law-abiding citizens who are the victims of crime. They could stand up and demand more adequate police protection and better-trained police forces. They could demand that the victims of crime be assured the services of an attorney, the same way criminals are.

Because they already have good medical-research departments, the life companies are in a particularly strong position to play a leading role in the struggle to free much of America's population from the pernicious grip of the avaricious narcotic peddlers. Here again, the insurance people should go into our schools and talk to the kids and give them straight and convincing information about the horrible perils of drugs.

What I have tried to say is that, for an industry that is so dependent on the good will of the multitudes, a more energetic approach to helping our entire population would be well advised. Such action can only endear the industry rather than have it totally castigated, as surely it will be if the do-nothing policy continues.

8. *The Heavy Grip of Inflation*

T HE 1974 *TREND REPORT* of the Institute of Life Insurance was more than a confession of past and current sins. Although it was drafted before price rises reached annual levels of twelve and thirteen percent under President Carter, it sounded the alarm that the industry was in grave danger from inflation.

The report said that solvency of the establishment companies was definitely threatened and that future operating costs would be unpredictable and unmanageable.

Unfortunately, inflation is worldwide, although less obvious in the communist countries than in the free-enterprise world.* That raises grave doubts whether any president can bring it under reasonable control in the next few years. The oil shortages, the untenable political situation in the Middle

---

* See Arthur Milton, *Will Inflation Destroy America?* (Secaucus, N.J.: Citadel Press, 1977).

East, and the clear indication that as a result of the Russian invasion of Afghanistan the *détente* between the Soviet Union and the West is over and the cold war will be resumed—all these elements combine to deal a *coup de grace* to efforts to curb inflation in the United States.

Over the long haul, the energy crisis can be solved. Coal gasification, both underground and after the coal is brought to the surface, coal liquefaction, shale-oil extraction, massive production of renewable supplies of vegetable petroleum and ethanol alcohols, the fast-breeder nuclear reactor (which breeds more fuel than it consumes), and some applications of solar energy will do the job. There may be some help from light chemistry, too. But these are frightfully expensive, and we may not realize much from them for ten to twenty years. Indeed, early efforts to make these programs work will aggravate inflation rather than help bring it under control.

The National Science Foundation issued a report on January 14, 1980, saying that although the global energy situation will cause difficulties for the United States, it need not slow the nation's long-term economic growth. But the foundation pointed out that we can hope for no miracles, that conservation must be our main defense, and that coal and nuclear fission must be relied on increasingly in the years ahead as natural petroleum becomes scarcer. Even though huge amounts of natural oil remain in the ground, much of it is inaccessible at any cost. The foundation study downgraded the outlook for solar energy substantially, saying that no ways to achieve economies of scale in producing it have been found or are likely to be soon, although the aggregate benefit of small solar-energy applications will be most useful.

Meanwhile, we are going to have to pay through the nose for gasoline, diesel fuel, and heating oil, and that will continue to run up the cost of housing, transportation, food, clothing—everything we require in our daily lives.

The Middle East situation is a drain on all the world except the communists, who profit by it. It is the prime cause of the high price and scarcity of oil. Of course, it can be said that the oil-exporting Arab countries are not being drained financially, but in reality they are. They maintain costly armaments, which they would not need if the Middle East crisis, now thirty years old, could be solved. But countries not directly involved in the conflict between Israel and the Arabs, such as Turkey and Greece and even Pakistan, have had their economies disrupted by the long confrontation. Turkey is in the grip of severe inflation and an even worse energy shortage, which keep her on the ragged edge of civil war.

Israel is undergoing fearful inflation—at the rate of 109 percent in 1979. The mess in Iran, including the seizure of the hostages, is actually only a skirmish in the Middle Eastern conflict, humiliating as it has been to Americans. In my opinion, the crux of the conflict is the demands of the Palestinians, which I do not think can be satisfied without destroying the state of Israel. Israel is not willing to commit suicide and the West is not willing to abandon Israel, but the communist countries and the more militant Muslim leaders seem determined to keep the conflict going until the end of this century.

The resumption of the cold war will run up American armament outlays and add to the difficulty of supporting the dollar and obtaining relief from inflation.

Despite its many gloomy prognostications for the future of life insurance, the *Trend Report* left out one of the most important reasons for pessimism. It failed to comment on the fact that the marvelous, almost miraculous scientific developments that helped the industry to prosper astoundingly in the years right after World War II are not likely to be duplicated in the remainder of the century.

The electronic-accounting revolution has not fully run its course, but the great cost- and labor-saving benefits to the life-insurance companies already have been realized. And although medicine, surgery, and pharmaceutical chemistry will continue to advance, progress is sure to be much slower than during the war years and postwar years that gave human-kind the antibiotic drugs and so many other blessings.

The consensus of opinion is that there is not going to be a breakthrough in treatment of cancer or cardiovascular diseases. There definitely is no single cause of cancer or heart diseases, and there will be no miraculous prevention or cure for either. So the life companies cannot expect another tremendous improvement in mortality experience and human lifespans, which would produce new profits and break the heavy grip of inflation for at least a decade or two.

A leveling off in population expansion also will limit the growth of the business.

Inflation's heavy bite on industry and commerce in general may seriously erode the investment income in other businesses, which is almost as important as policy revenues to the life companies.

The most dangerous characteristic of the current inflation is its persistence. During the second term of President Nixon, we hoped that the close of the Vietnam war would bring an end to inflation and possibly a beneficial deflation, but that did not happen. In a very real sense, today's inflation is worse than the galloping inflation that ravaged Germany, France, Italy, and Austria in the early 1920s. Fantastic as the fall of those countries' currencies then was, the critical period was brief, and it was followed by years of relative monetary stability. But there seems to be no hope of stability anywhere on the horizon today.

With a dry casualness, the *Trend Report* says, "The rate of inflation will abort thrift as an achievable goal in the minds of the public."

What do these stilted words really imply?

They imply the widespread death of the hope of laying up anything for the future and the total or nearly total destruction of the American way of working and saving. Our rate of saving has already fallen below that of the populaces of virtually all other industrialized countries. These words reflect a fear or at least a cynical belief that most Americans will turn to day-to-day opportunism or, like the people of so many underdeveloped countries, will come to believe that a government job is the only sure way of making a comfortable living. No matter how you gloss it over, holding a government job means living off money sweated out of the taxpayers; it means the opposite of being productive.

Professor Paul Pfeiffer, of Kent State University in Ohio, commented on one aspect of the problem in an address to the 1979 annual conference of the Life Management Society. He said that the 1980s would bring many employment problems for the life companies. He said that workers would want faster promotion and a bigger voice in management decisions but then added somewhat pessimistically, "Yet their demands won't always coincide with commitment to greater quality work."

The *Trend Report* had plenty to say about employee relations. It said that inflation will force curbs on fringe benefits for workers and the pressure for shorter working hours will abate. It said that the companies will have to follow different

philosophies in dealing with clerical and professional workers. The professional workers, being highly mobile and able
to switch readily from company to company, will be interested
in compensation solely on the basis of merit, the report said,
but for clerical and other "inferior workers," it said, "the
focus will be on cost-of-living incentives."

The report warned, though, that raising the compensation of "inferior" workers because of inflation's impact on
the cost of living is sure to lead to discontent and a lack of
motivation on the part of the "superior" workers. That's a
classic inflation dilemma that is being aggravated this time
because the inflation is so persistent.

This is not hard to understand. We have drained all
motivation out of tens of millions of our workers and have
eliminated their self-respect over the last twenty-five years
through giveaway programs that include unreasonable benefits in poverty checks, food stamps, and unemployment insurance on excessively easy terms.

We have seen in the previous chapters that many agents
view with dismay the manner in which inflation is causing a
shift from whole-life to term insurance. They will have to
sell a lot more death insurance to many more customers to
make the same living, especially since inflation is also running up their living costs and their office and sales costs.

The *Trend Report* says that there will have to be some
radical changes in the compensation of agents. It suggests,
for example, that some of the indexed-commission-schedule
methods used for property and casualty insurance could be
adapted to life insurance and that perhaps salary should be
a bigger portion of agents' compensation. On the indexing,
the *Trend Report* suggests, "The type of indexing currently
used for casualty coverage (such as regular or intermittent

offers to increase homeowners' insurance as property values go up; the decrease in collision coverage as auto values go down) could be used for life insurance, possibly without the direct intervention of the agent, thus obviating the need for a full front-end (commission) load."

Another suggestion, put rather vaguely in the report, is for salaried agents.

However, it seems plain that an energetic, well-informed agent can do a lot to cope with the changing picture just by trying to make sure that his or her customers have as much death protection as they need and can afford. The need for death protection increases at least as fast as the inflation of money. I have before me a couple of tables by two fairly good life companies showing how much additional death protection a family now needs just to keep up with inflation, without regard to growing family needs.

Here's how much additional life insurance you may need to keep pace with what inflation has done to the value of the dollar.

Year You Last Bought Insurance	Average Consumer Price Index for That Year	If You Bought $100,000 of Insurance, You Now Need an Additional	Percentage of Additional Coverage Needed
1967	100.0	$146,500	146.5
1968	104.2	136,600	136.6
1969	109.8	124,500	124.5
1970	116.3	112,000	112.0
1971	121.3	103,200	103.2
1972	125.3	96,700	96.7
1973	133.1	85,200	85.2
1974	147.7	66,900	66.9
1975	161.2	52,900	52.9
1976	170.5	44,600	44.6
1977	181.5	35,800	35.8
1978	195.4	26,200	26.2
1979	217.4	13,400	13.4
1980	246.5*	—	—

* Based upon U.S. Department of Labor statistics and a forecast of 1980.

The more dramatic of the two tables gives the following percentages of additional coverage needed at the start of 1980 on a policy bought in each of the past thirteen years.

This means that if a person bought $100,000 worth of insurance in 1967, he or she needs $146,500 of *additional* insurance today, just to keep up with inflation.

We already have pointed out that most couples in their prime years need at least $30,000 to $100,000 worth of term death coverage. A family that needed and could afford $100,000 worth of insurance in 1967 may very well now need —and be able to afford—$246,500 worth if proper term death insurance is purchased.

Life-insurance people also worry, with good cause, lest some consumers decide in these inflationary days to be "self-insured," that is, to depend on their ability to save and invest their money for a maximum return instead of buying insurance. If you have been brainwashed into thinking of life insurance primarily as a way of saving, that would seem to make a lot of sense. But life insurance is not a way of saving. As I keep pointing out, it is death insurance. With proper term insurance, a couple with young children can accumulate an immediate $50,000 or $100,000 estate for the family, if the breadwinner dies. There is simply no way this family could create such an estate by putting money in the bank and making a few modest investments.

This is where an honest independent agent is worth her or his weight in gold. Honest advice on financial planning for the future of your family and yourself is covered in detail in Chapter 12.

Unless the life companies adapt more rapidly than they have so far to the troubles caused by inflation, some of them are going to go under. The state insurance commissioners will probably compel the stronger companies to take over policies of companies facing collapse. That has been done for many years. Fortunately, as pointed out in chapter 3, most states now protect policyholders. But the stockholders and employees and many agents of the failing companies could be wiped out.

9. *The Bear Market Is Here*

IN THE 1940s AND 1950s, some people made large profits by investing in the stocks of life-insurance companies, because the business expanded so much in those years and the profitability was enhanced by a large increase in the average life-span in America.

But even in the years when the business was having its greatest growth, the stocks of life companies required great patience on the part of investors if substantial rewards were to be reaped.

Although the shares of some of the big multi-line insurance companies are listed and traded on the New York Stock Exchange and a few life companies are listed on the American Stock Exchange, the typical life-insurance company is closely held, and the minority shares in the hands of the public are traded over the counter. The market for these shares is usually somewhat thinner than the market for shares of industrial companies traded over the counter. That makes the life stocks

rather volatile and unsuited for the investor who wants to
speculate on short term profits—the person who maintains
what is called in Wall Street a trading account with his or her
brokerage house, as distinguished from an investment account.

The unsuitability of life-insurance-company stocks for
quick sale without the risk of a substantial markdown also
makes them somewhat difficult to borrow money on at the
bank. If you put up a hundred shares of General Motors or
some other respectable industrial stock as collateral for a
loan, the bank knows it can get its money in a matter of hours
or even minutes should you default. But it might have to wait
days to sell and collect on life stocks, and the borrower would
probably take a loss, and the bank might lose some of its
money.

Also, life-insurance-company shares have never been
considered income stocks. As a rule, they pay very modest
cash dividends or no dividends.

So stock life-insurance companies have traditionally
paid dividends in stock, rather than cash. Thus, the only way
the buyer of the shares can reap cash from them is to sell off
his dividend shares from time to time or to sell his holdings
as their book value appreciates or to get paid for them as the
result of a merger or acquisition of the company. So the life
stocks have been called growth stocks, and their market value
has depended on book value, which is arrived at by dividing
the number of shares outstanding into the sum that the balance sheet indicates could be reasonably raised if the company's assets and business were sold.

A big attraction of all growth stocks is that if you make
any profit by selling them, the profit is taxed as capital gains,
rather than straight income, and taxes on capital gains are

usually much lower than income taxes. In recent years, however, Congress has shown an inclination to raise the capital-gains tax rates, and that could make life-insurance stocks and other growth stocks less attractive.

In the sixteen years since the prices of life stocks peaked out and began to decline in 1964, their performance as growth stocks has left much to be desired, and there are indications that we may indeed be in for a real bear market for life stocks.

In his New York's outlook statement for 1980, Blake Newton, president of the American Council of Life Insurance, tried to sound very optimistic about the prospects of the life companies even as he depicted the ravages of inflation and the horrible black clouds on the international political horizon. Newton predicted that the average amount of family life-insurance protection would rise in 1980 by the same rate as in 1979, when it climbed $3,500, to $44,300. That was an increase of 8.58 percent, but inflation for 1979 was 13 percent, so the life companies were not keeping up with inflation in this important respect. Also, a large part of that $44,300 average family coverage had to be group term insurance, not the high-priced whole-life insurance that earned such big profits for the life companies in the 1940s and 1950s.

Mr. Newton also said that the life companies should add forty billion dollars to the flow of investment cash available to the country's economy in 1980, an increase of four billion dollars from the 1979 gain in this respect. That's an increase of about 11.1 percent, but it's still below what inflation ran for the year—a fact Newton didn't mention.

Let us contrast Newton's somewhat forced optimism with a forecast on the prospects for the life companies during the 1980s made by the prestigious Chase Econometrics Group, of Bala Cynwyd, Pennsylvania, a firm owned by New York's Chase Manhattan Corporation.

Written by David Hemley, the Chase Study said,

> The life industry already has problems with the mix of life policies shifting toward more term insurance and less whole life insurance. At present this situation is exacerbated by high inflation and especially by high interest rates as increasingly sophisticated consumers reject whole life as a savings vehicle in favor of other savings instruments.
>
> The economic recession we are now entering represents one more turn of the screw for the life industry. As the unemployment rate soars to 8 percent by the end of 1980, the recession will impact most heavily on the manufacturing industries, causing widespread layoffs and keeping manufacturing employment flat for the next nine months. Those industries are the most unionized and offer the richest market for comprehensive group life policies. But that market will not grow in real terms for another year or so.
>
> Our forecasts indicate that premium growth for the life industry will slow down—in current dollars—for the next two years. When inflation is figured in, premium revenues in the life industry will actually show a decline.

Hemley said that demographics also show that the life-insurance market will be declining during the next few years. He added,

> As the market shrinks, the pressure on individual companies to maintain market share will grow, which will increase price cutting—in an industry where the cost of coverage per thousand dollars already is falling in absolute terms . . . companies will have to be increasingly vigilant in monitoring losses and expenses if they are to avoid a serious profitability squeeze.

A new organization called the American Association of Individual Investors, formed in Chicago to foster the interests of the little investor in a stock market dominated by large institutional traders and investors, took a rather bearish view of the stock market's overall prospects for the 1980s, although conceding that the market had held up better in 1979 than might have been expected.

But there now appear to be some comparatively new reasons for concluding that a bear market in life-insurance stocks will remain with us for some time.

In the first place, we can see the working out of many of the difficulties forecast under Scenario 1 of the 1974 *Trend Report* of the Institute of Life Insurance.

Next, inflation obviously hurts the life-insurance business more than it hurts other businesses. The life companies cannot raise prices to match inflation as manufacturers and producers of raw materials and commodities can, for the simple reason that they have been overcharging their customers for years and the inflation catches them at a time when the consumerist movement and competition are forcing them to cut prices. Their only resort is to sell more and that can be a big order. The easiest way to sell more is to diversify into property and casualty insurance and investment instruments, but that entails much effort and acquiring much new knowledge and experience on the part of sales organizations.

Happily, many independent insurance agents have already acquired the necessary knowledge and experience. The Money Doctor, more fully described in chapter 12, will become more and more a valuable asset to many insurance companies.

Another reason this is not a good moment to invest in

life stocks is that so many of the best companies, the real plums, have been swallowed up in mergers and acquisitions in the past few years. They have mostly been bought for stock, and the acquisition cost has diluted the shares of the purchasing companies and weakened their potential as growth stocks.

The life companies have successfully blocked the Federal Trade Commission for the moment from further investigation of their business but, the demands from consumerists for tighter regulation are rising. That is a threat to the value of life stocks that could choke off new investor interest.

Perhaps the most serious single problem for the companies was stated succinctly, even though he did not elaborate much on it, by Professor Paul Pfeiffer, of Kent State University, when he said that it is likely to be very difficult to motivate life-insurance agents and employees in the 1980s. Michael Lynch, chief of the group of economists who worked on the controversial FTC staff report, took a similar view. He said that the people who may be the most shocked by an effective disclosure system could be the army of agents working for the establishment companies. He said that many of these agents may revolt when they learn that the companies have been requiring or inducing them to sell outmoded products for so many years.

The fact that the big mutual companies still have such a large share of the market and are stronger financially in general than the stock life companies could also seriously hurt the prospects for the life stocks. In the booming forties and fifties, the stock companies greatly improved their share of the market, but that was mainly because they were able, through high-pressure selling and innovative policy designing, to expand the overall market rapidly. In a market that is not expanding rapidly, competing with the mutuals could be much harder, especially since the mutuals have been encroaching on the stock companies' own turf.

The number of life-insurance companies may be reduced from the present eighteen hundred to no more than six hundred during the 1980s. This grim possibility is raised in a recent study by Robert Posnak, a partner in Ernst and Whitney, an accounting firm that audits about twenty-five percent of the life-insurance industry.

Posnak said that many of the smaller companies are very marginal, but those which have carved specialties for themselves may survive; the others will be taken over by bigger companies. He also said that pressure for more regulation of the business will speed the shakeout. The companies' whole-life-insurance business will inevitably decline, he said, and there will be ever-sharper attacks by consumerists on such profitable fields as credit life insurance and industrial life insurance—that is, small policies sold at high rates on monthly payments.

He predicted that the criticism of credit life insurance will force regulations that will give borrowers a better break and will therefore reduce the profits the insurors and the banks and finance companies make on this business.

10. *The Industry's Mistakes*

FROM ITS EARLIEST DAYS, the life-insurance industry has been less willing than other businesses to admit its
mistakes. Having adopted a posture of being marvelous new
benefactors of humankind, its leaders felt bound to assume
a mystique of infallibility such as the leaders of religions
often feel compelled to profess.

Of course, the truth is quite different. The business was
founded in an era of brutal *caveat-emptor* economics, and
the Brahmans who run the establishment life companies in
the United States have attempted to maintain this "let the
buyer beware" philosophy well into the last quarter of the
twentieth century.

Most of the industry's errors have been at the expense
of the insurance-buying public, but not altogether so. Waste-
ful management and extravagance and bad judgment in investments can be as harmful to life-company stockholders as
to policyholders. It is the duty of state regulatory officials to

look for such abuses and expose them. They do this a little more frequently than is generally realized, but actual prosecution occurs only in the more flagrant cases, and many insurance people believe that the establishment companies are dealt with leniently. On the other hand, agents can be subjected to considerable regulatory harassment if they behave in a way that is offensive to the establishment.

One of the earliest mistakes of the industry was to encourage the sale of life insurance on children. In an age when childhood diseases caused high mortality rates, it was easy to sell parents on the idea of insurance that would at least pay the funeral expenses when a child died. And there was the added sales argument that an early policy would give the child lifelong insurability protection.

This backfired. Childhood mortality rates and suspicious deaths of children went up surprisingly on both sides of the Atlantic. The losses to the companies were heavy. That did not stop the companies from pushing the sale of insurance for children; it only made them sell more selectively. As late as the early 1930s, millions of families burdened themselves to buy whole life insurance on their children instead of purchasing death insurance for the father, the family breadwinner. Even endowment policies for children were sold on the idea that they would come due and be paid off in time to provide useful funds in the critical young-adult years. The truth, of course, is that even then there were vastly better ways to save money for children than buying such expensive life-insurance policies on them.

Greed and duplicity have been the life-insurance industry's greatest sins. Sins are mistakes; in church and synagogue, congregations confess in their prayers, "We have erred grievously in thy sight, O Lord." As early as 1877, Elizur Wright, a Massachusetts mathematician who later became the state's first insurance commissioner, wrote a little book entitled *Traps Baited with Orphans.* Wright exposed the shortcomings of whole-life cash-value insurance roundly and concluded, "I became convinced that life insurance was the most available, convenient and permanent breeding place for rogues that civilization ever had presented."

That things haven't changed altogether since Wright's day could be inferred from a recent popular detective novel. The villain in the story is a vice-president of a life-insurance company. Early on, he remarks rather cheerfully to a claims investigator, "[Owning] a life insurance company is a license to steal."

One of the worst examples of company greed that betrays the uninformed policyholder into making serious mistakes is the policy loan. Instead of conceding you the right to withdraw some of the surplus premiums you have paid on a whole-life cash-value policy, the companies pretend that they are lending you money and charge you interest on it. They get away with this, and state insurance codes actually define this withdrawal of your own money as a loan. At present the companies are moaning that the interest rates on these loans aren't high enough, and we saw in the chapter on the 1974 *Trend Report* that they were even talking of welshing on guarantees of loan-interest rates written into the new policies.

A couple of years ago, the establishment companies prevailed on state insurance commissions to increase interest on loans made to policyholders (of their own money) from an average of five percent to eight percent. With few exceptions, industry executives flocked together and, regardless of the impact on the public, followed the lead in carrying out this outrageous imposition.

It use to be much more sensible most of the time for the policyholder to borrow money elsewhere rather than from the insurance company. At least he or she would be getting the use of extra funds instead of paying for the privilege of using his or her own money. But probably, policy loans are usually taken out because the insured is in no position to borrow from a bank or finance company at the moment.

On the whole, policy loans have been fabulously profitable to life companies. In times when bank and finance-company rates were low, interest rates on life-insurance-policy loans were comparatively high.

Careless selection and poor training of salespeople is a mistake the life-insurance business has made in common with many other businesses. For years most or many salespeople rose from the ranks of the debit or industrial-life forces. This is the business of ringing doorbells, or visiting factories during lunch hours, to sell small policies of a few hundred dollars to the lowest-income workers, to be paid for by the month. The salespeople build up collectible accounts called debits and have to call every month and collect the small premiums themselves.

Their customers are not sophisticated, and it is not at all hard to sell them small amounts of insurance at rates three and a half to five times as high as the rates that would be quoted middle-class life-insurance prospects. Over the years there have been many exposés of industrial life insurance but it still goes on. For many years this was almost the only life insurance available to blacks, and I am told that in the Deep South it was called bluntly "nigger insurance." As was the case (and still is sometimes) with other commodities and services, the poor blacks were charged several times as much for paltry insurance protection as upper-working-class and middle-class whites would pay for much better protection.

This debit insurance is not sold by small, disreputable companies as a rule. The greater part of the business is written by the big establishment companies.

Salespeople trained in that rapacious and cynical field were not likely to become oversolicitous about policyholders or too squeamish about gouging them for every penny of commissions they could squeeze from them.

Things have improved in recent years. Agents are somewhat better trained, but the training is still aimed at maximizing commission earnings and company profit, not at giving policyholders maximum death protection for their survivors for the least money.*

Stringent underwriting has caused many persons to buy "rated" policies because of supposed health or occupational perils, forcing them to pay extra dollars in premiums over the years. These rated health and occupational hazards have been shown to be highly overrated and not to justify so much in premiums. But the companies have not made any effort to rectify these ratings and reduce the premiums—another industry mistake that will arouse public resentment.

The duplicity of the life companies was most glaring in the arcane language in which they wrote their policies, language so obfuscating that even an attorney could not comprehend it unless he or she had specialized in insurance law. The insured had to take their agents' word for what the policy

* See Arthur Milton, *How to Get a Dollar's Value for a Dollar Spent* (Secaucus, N.J.: Citadel Press, 1964).

said, and there were plenty of occasions when a beneficiary learned that the policy did not say what the agent had pretended it did when he or she sold it. Not until the early 1970s did harsh criticism from many quarters force a few of the companies to start writing their life policies in plain English. Before this, even the sales organizations had often not known how to read the policies.

Life-insurance companies can be extremely alert and forward looking when new opportunities develop for profit, either in selling policies with new wrinkles to the public or in making investments with handsome yield potental. But they show a curiously ostrich-like attitude toward really important and widespread social changes. It seems to me that the establishment companies have kept their heads buried in the sand for the past fifteen years while the tides of consumerism rose all around them and threatened ultimately to engulf them completely.

They keep on stubbornly increasing their efforts to maintain expensive sales forces devoted to selling products that not only are outdated but, in many cases, should never have been offered for sale in the first place.

But from the standpoint of both the public and the insurance agents, the worst mistakes of the companies have been to frustrate legitimate regulation of the industry by the states. They have effectively pigeonholed the state insurance laws and turned them and the state insurance officials largely into instruments to protect the companies instead of the public.

The most glaring example of this is the way the anti-twisting rules have been turned into means of locking policyholders into high-cost cash-value insurance policies that no longer serve the needs of the insured but still earn fat profits for the companies. The states originally adopted the anti-twisting rules to stop agents from shifting policies from company to company or even shifting customers to other policies in the same company just to generate fat commissions. This practice was analogous to unscrupulous stockbrokers' "churning" customers' stock portfolios in order to generate commissions.

But as the public became better informed and the number of sophisticated independent insurance agents increased, the companies persuaded the state insurance departments to turn the anti-twisting rules into newer, tougher "replacement regulations" designed to make it more difficult for a private individual to change her or his insurance and to make it unprofitable and even illegal and dangerous for an agent to help a customer get out of a bad life-insurance situation and into a good one.

Suppose John Appleseed, who lives in New York State, has a hundred thousand dollars' worth of very old cash value insurance written at a time when mortality experience was a lot poorer than it is now, investment-income prospects were not as good, and premiums were much higher. He asks his independent agent what to do.

The agent knows full well that he can get Appleseed a hundred thousand dollars' worth of term insurance for not more than one-sixth of what he is paying now, all things considered. The cash-value policy or policies can be cashed in for, say, fifteen thousand dollars, and this sum can be put in a savings bank or otherwise invested to earn 11 or 12 percent, as against the yield from the cash-value policy on premiums paid in of from 1½ to 4 percent.

But because of Regulation 60 of the New York State Department of Insurance, put into effect in October 1971, the agent is going to be awfully wary about advising Appleseed to take this sensible step. The commission on the new arrangement for Appleseed might be less than $150, and Regulation 60 forces the agent to go through complicated steps that eat up much of the commission in clerical costs. Also, if he makes a small mistake, or even if he merely incurs the displeasure of the company that now insures Appleseed or its agent, he can be harassed and fined by the state insurance department and even have his license revoked.

As a former insurance commissioner once told me, this regulation is the biggest vote for high-cost insurance ever perpetrated on the public by the establishment.

Ever since the replacement problem began nibbling at the entrenched privileges of the establishment companies, they have been putting pressure on all state insurance departments to adopt similar rules. They have succeeded in virtually all the states. This has been done very quietly. These tough new rules haven't had to be voted on by the state legislatures, and hardly anyone outside the industry knows about them. Only a handful of agents so far have been willing to stick their necks out and protest.

The antireplacement rules are all preceded by pious declarations that they are designed to protect the public, but if you ask a *former* state insurance official about it, the chances are he or she will tell you bluntly that the rules are designed to protect the companies, not the public. Of course, these regulations also say that a private individual can change his or her insurance if he or she wants to, but there are some big catches to that. It is difficult, almost impossible, to buy standard term life insurance at reasonable prices without going through an agent, and you usually have to prove that you are still medically insurable. If you cash in your existing insurance first so you can buy new insurance without going through complicated "replacement" procedures, you are left in the meanwhile without death protection, and there is the risk that you might be turned down medically for the replacement insurance.

To give you an idea of how ridiculous the regulation is, it talks about the suicide clause and the contestable period you would have in a new policy that you don't have in the old policy. Generally, the suicide and contestable clauses run for two years and then expire. Can you imagine that the combined genius of the life-insurance executives and state insurance officials has caused them to conclude that you might commit suicide in the next two years or you will commit fraud in your application for the new policy? How sad it is that these attitudes have served to make the public even more wary of the life companies.

As a rule, the tough replacement regulations don't apply to group insurance, insurance issued as part of a pension plan, or nonrenewable term insurance. But the New York rule applies to "any replacement transaction which involves annuity contracts except those provisions which require the completion and furnishing of a disclosure statement."

New York Regulation 60 is a fourteen-page document that ends with a dozen detailed admonitions that must be given to applicants who want to change their insurance, warning them that doing so is nearly always a bad thing. It is a defense of whole-life cash-value insurance all the way and doesn't contain a single phrase about the advantages of term insurance or the need for a maximum death benefit. The agent is required to furnish this document to people like John Appleseed.

The agent is also required by Regulation 60 to fill out a whole series of disclosure forms listing all Appleseed's life-insurance policies, the policy numbers, the companies' names and addresses, the face amounts, the various benefits and options, and the premium rates, with tables of dividend and cash-value prospects for each policy for many years hence. The agent also must give specific reasons for dropping each old policy and specify the advantages to be obtained by purchasing the new policy. These forms must be signed by both the agent and Appleseed. Copies of them must be sent to all the insurance companies involved, as well as to all the other life-insurance agents Appleseed has dealt with. All this runs into time and money.

Regulation 60 also provides severe penalties for any agent for "counselling of the insured to write directly to the company in such a way as to bypass such company's agency representation or obscure the identity of the replacing agents and company."

In the closing statement's admonitions that have to be given to Appleseed, Regulation 60 contains this advice: "For your protection, you should receive the comments of the present insurance company before arriving at a decision on this important financial matter."

Possibly, but if Appleseed drives a Ford and decides to trade it in on a Chevrolet, would state officials presume to tell him he should ask the advice of the Ford Motor Company and the state motor-vehicle department before closing the deal?

The establishment life companies would doubtless answer that you don't buy an automobile to keep for life and expect it to increase in value. But in this inflationary era we have seen that old life-insurance policies lose their value, and the companies admit that. But more important, the average life of a life-insurance policy that stays in effect is now less than the average life of a good automobile.

So Regulation 60 and rules like it in other states seem more and more like arbitrary abuses of regulatory power to aid and protect the life-insurance establishment.

11. *The Disclosure Fiasco*

IN 1975, THE NEWS MAGAZINE *U.S. News & World Report* published a wide-ranging study of American opinion. One of the conclusions it published was that only about nineteen percent of those queried said they thought the life-insurance companies deserved a good rating for providing the public with information.

Considering the large public-relations and publicity efforts the industry has mounted all through this century, that was a rather devastating verdict. It implied that the life companies' boasted disclosures about their business look to the public like a fraud.

Is it because executives of life companies have acted holier than thou and have always felt that they were running charitable institutions, which, in fact, they have not been doing at all?

The companies practice bold deceptions. I spoke about the gall of the companies in making you pay interest on your own money when you take out a policy loan. But if you don't take out a loan and continue to pay level premiums on a cash-value policy, you pay the same price year after year for less and less death insurance. Suppose you have a twenty-thousand-dollar policy that costs five hundred a year. The first year you paid five hundred for twenty thousand dollars' worth of death protection. But suppose that now your policy has accumulated eight thousand dollars in cash value. You are really paying five hundred per year now for only twelve thousand dollars' worth of death protection. This is rarely disclosed by a captive agent selling the policy. In fact, he or she may even mislead the applicant into thinking the survivor will get the twenty thousand dollars *plus* the accumulated cash values if the applicant dies, which isn't the case. She or he will get twenty thousand dollars, less any loan the insured may have taken out on the policy.

In 1970, the Life Underwriters Training Council and the Life Agency Management Association published a study based on interviews in 1968 and 1969 with about 1,750 recently widowed women. It was called *The Widows Study*.

Although ninety-two percent of the widows said that their husbands had had some kind of life insurance, seventy percent got death benefits of less than ten thousand dollars and fifty-two percent less than five thousand dollars. Only seven percent received monthly payments under policy options. Yet forty-seven percent of these widows had dependent children. Half of them said their standards of living had dropped fairly sharply after their husbands died. This pathetic showing reveals something radically wrong with the business of life insurance.

Perhaps the most remarkable discovery in the study was that only twenty percent of these women had seriously discussed life insurance with their husbands or the insurance agent and many of them had had no idea how much insurance there was in the family until the husband and father died.

Of course, in the decade since that study, things have changed. The working wife is the rule in America now, and the life-insurance companies, who fifty years ago were extremely reluctant to insure females, are eagerly trying to sell them policies, because on the average, women live about seven years longer than men. So women know a lot more about life insurance, and husbands nowadays rarely make a life-insurance decision without telling their wives all the details and asking their advice.

This improvement doesn't excuse the cruel hoax that the life-insurance establishment perpetrated on people for a hundred and twenty-five years in pretending that whole-life cash-value insurance generally provided anything substantial for a man's wife and children if he died young. This was the first great disclosure fiasco of the industry.

What I am getting at is simply that the cost of ten thousand dollars' worth of whole-life insurance is almost the same as the cost of a hundred thousand dollars' worth of term insurance, and probably the latter is what the industry always should have offered the public. This is even more true today, because as I have already revealed, taxation and inflation have made it hard enough for most folk to make ends meet. They just about have enough dollars left for pure, unadulterated death (term) insurance.

In the last chapter we described another disclosure fiasco, the antireplacement regulations that employ complicated so-called disclosure procedures to lock policyholders into bad insurance situations and tie the hands of independent agents who want to help the policyholders.

The conflict between the disclosure plan on true life-insurance-policy costs proposed in the 1979 FTC staff report and the disclosure plan drafted by the National Association of Insurance Commissioners was described in chapter 4. Peter Spielman and Aaron Zelman say in their book *The Life Insurance Conspiracy* that "the NAIC plan is so weak it is laughable."

It does not require furnishing any real comparative figures; only the cost figures for the policy being sold must be given, and this information is provided only after the customer signs the application.

After getting several states to adopt the NAIC disclosure plan, the life-insurance lobby in Washington succeeded in 1978 in getting both House and Senate appropriations committees to put in the budget appropriation for the FTC these words: "the committee directs that in no event should the Commission or its staff attempt to impede or thwart the adoption by the states of the model life insurance cost solicitation regulation supported by the NAIC."

That tied the FTC staff's hands only through fiscal 1979. The controversial staff report was issued around the end of the fiscal year, and we have seen how the insurance industry then turned to tie the hands of the FTC staff again by getting the Senate Commerce Committee to adopt the Cannon insurance amendment to the McCarran-Ferguson Act.

Life-insurance policies are sometimes sold for the specific purpose of offsetting estate taxes, and this is sometimes advantageous, but the agent should point out that for most married couples it's not likely to be necessary because of the marital deduction under the estate-tax law. This deduction is fifty percent of the adjusted estate, that is, the gross estate less debts and legitimate expenses, or $250,000, whichever is greater.

Perhaps the worst disclosure fiasco is the idea harped on in much life-insurance-company propaganda that many persons lack the discipline to save their money themselves and the insurance companies are doing them a great favor by saving it for them—for a price. Even in days when people were not as well educated as now, there was very little truth in this propaganda. It is natural for people to save. The rustic who buried his money in the ground in a crock was acting out of ignorance and distrust of his fellows. The farmer's wife who kept her butter-and-egg money in a paper bag buried in the sugar jar was being foolish. But they both saved. And even in the nineteenth century there were savings banks, building-and-loan associations, and other thrift institutions where people could deposit their savings and have them grow and earn much more than a life-insurance policy could accumulate.

Today the small-savings opportunities are numerous, and the poorest of them return a much better yield than a cash-value life-insurance policy.

The significant thing is that people have always demonstrated their eagerness to save. All they needed was opportunity and information. Even illiterate Americans would save to buy a little piece of land and put a house on it, or to get a horse or a cow or a piece of farm machinery. As people became more sophisticated, they learned how to borrow from banks for these things and how to plan to make them earn much more than enough to pay off the loans.

The measure of Americans' ability to save on their own is the vast diversity and volume of savings.

Inflation, the gasoline shortage, and disruption in business reduced the reported savings of Americans sharply in 1979 to 4.5 percent of personal disposable income, or about $72.8 billion out of $1.623 trillion. In most years of the 1970s and 1960s, the savings rate was around 7.5 percent. Personal disposable income is roughly take-home pay, what's left after the bite for income taxes and Social Security. That 1979 personal-disposable-income figure is out of a gross national product exceeding $2 trillion. So after paying for other taxes, food, shelter, clothing, transportation, fuel, health care, straight insurance of all kinds, interest on loans, and other necessities, Americans put away in thrift institutions and thrift funds a recorded $72.8 billion in 1979. It was not a good showing. In 1975, Americans saved $83.6 billion, or 7.7 percent of disposable income, and the dollar bought considerably more in 1975 than in 1979.

But the net-savings figure is an understatement of how much Americans really save or try to save. They actually deposit at least fifty percent more in various thrift accounts and funds, but circumstances compel them to withdraw substantial sums. For example, occasionally the savings-bank association will report a net deposit outflow for a month or so, and it is well-known that although the sales of the federal government's Series E savings bonds are quite large, many of them are cashed in after the required holding period of two months.

People also save through Christmas savings clubs and similar devices. Purchases of annuities, mutual funds, and investments (as distinguished from outright speculation) in stocks and bonds come largely out of savings.

There's another side to the story: We now have in the

United States, as a result of inflation, an "underground" economy that some good economists think is at least one-third as large as the recorded economy. The personal savings that grow out of this underground economy go highly unrecorded and are at a higher percentage of income than the recorded savings because they so frequently escape being taxed. If we could include the savings growing out of the underground economy in the national personal-savings statistics, it is fairly certain the figure would be much higher than the 4.5 percent figure reported for 1979.

That 4.5 percent is a sorry figure, one of the lowest current rates of any developed country, and it says volumes about the careless economic policies we have been following as a nation in recent years. But even that figure is so big that it demonstrates the total falsehood of propaganda that people need a life-insurance company to stand over them and make them save.

Another disclosure failure is the neglect of the life companies to tell their agents or even the agency supervisors the whole truth about the industry or even about the company they are working for.

Many universities now have professors who teach insurance as an important part of business economics, and considerable about it is taught in the better high schools. In spite of this, some surveys made by life-insurance trade groups in recent years have shown that fully half of all agents and probably a much higher proportion of captive agents have totally erroneous ideas about the true nature of the business. One fairly extensive study made by the National Association of Life Underwriters and the Life Insurance Marketing and Research Association found that thirty-seven percent of all full-time agents believe there is little or no difference between companies in the prices of similar policies, and another eleven per cent said they didn't know anything about that.

Worse, the study showed that the supervisors were worse informed than the agents. Forty-five percent of the supervisors opined that there was very little difference in similar-policy premium costs, and eleven percent said that they said they didn't know.

This flies right in the face of the demonstrable fact that no industry in America has such a widely varied, chaotic, and inexplicable pricing structure as life insurance.

If the agents and supervisors don't know the truth, how can they possibly disclose it to the public?

The enormous public-relations and publicity effort of the life-insurance business is carried on by both the individual companies and trade associations. Many of these activities are on a high plane and well done. Statistical information is gathered regularly and made available to the government and to educational and scientific bodies.

This information is voluminous and reliable. The health-research and vital-statistics reports of the industry are particularly good. So are the statistics on the industry's growth and profitability, gross benefits payments, investment income, and contribution to national capital formation.

But this avalanche of information is only another disclosure fiasco when it comes to telling the average family what it really needs to know about life insurance, how to get the most and best death protection for the least money, and how to avoid being sold a policy that turns out to be an expensive lemon and getting locked into it.

12. *The Heart of the Matter*

I CAN SAY WITHOUT HESITATION that no two people think alike, no two people earn income exactly alike, and certainly no two people spend their money alike. The insurance business has fallen down horribly by not training its extensive sales organizations to advise people on the broad matter of money as it pertains to all individuals.

Now I must come to the big question—what should people in the prime of life do about creating an immediate estate by insurance and an ultimate estate by saving and investing?

Obviously, the second half of my question requires answers far beyond the scope of this book, but I can point to a sound start at achieving a satisfactory answer.

In simplest terms, the couple should create an immediate estate by means of term life insurance and plan for an ultimate estate by means of tax-deferred annuities, savings-bank accounts, and perhaps investments in stocks and bonds and real estate.

Male, age 35 - - - Face Amount: $100,000

Age	Year	Annual Whole Life Premium	Yearly Renewable Term Premium	Difference	Compounded at 12.25%
35	1	1,530	192	1,338	1,502
36	2	1,530	205	1,325	3,173
37	3	1,530	221	1,309	5,031
38	4	1,530	238	1,292	7,098
39	5	1,530	257	1,273	9,396
40	6	1,530	279	1,251	11,952
41	7	1,530	300	1,230	14,796
42	8	1,530	321	1,209	17,966
43	9	1,530	346	1,184	21,496
44	10	1,530	376	1,154	25,425
45	11	1,530	407	1,123	29,800
46	12	1,530	454	1,076	34,658
47	13	1,530	503	1,027	40,056
48	14	1,530	556	974	46,056
49	15	1,530	613	917	52,728
50	16	1,530	671	859	60,151
51	17	1,530	727	803	68,421
52	18	1,530	784	746	77,640
53	19	1,530	845	685	87,920
54	20	1,530	914	616	99,381
55	21	1,530	995	535	112,156
56	22	1,530	1,086	444	126,394
57	23	1,530	1,185	345	142,264
58	24	1,530	1,296	234	159,954
59	25	1,530	1,420	110	179,672
60	26	1,530	1,559	(29)	201,649
61	27	1,530	1,710	(180)	226,149
62	28	1,530	1,874	(344)	253,466
63	29	1,530	2,054	(524)	283,928
64	30	1,530	2,257	(727)	317,893

This chart indicates that if you purchased a whole-life cash-value policy at the age of thirty-five, the premium would be $1,530 yearly. The yearly renewable term premium is indicated. The difference is invested at the current rate being paid on a tax-deferred annuity. You will note that in twenty years the side fund (annuity) is already valued at almost $100,000; thus, the actual need for life insurance may no longer exist. Continuing an analysis of this table, owing to the benefits of compound interest (tax deferred), taking the difference in premium over the thirty-year period one can have an ultimate accumulation of almost $318,000 at age sixty-five, if current interest rates remain during the next thirty years. One can hardly justify not using this method of creating an immediate estate. Although the whole-life cash-value policy does develop cash values, they are lost in the event of death. But if you purchase term insurance and have the side fund also, the death benefit at any given year is the $100,000 of life insurance plus the accumulation in the side fund. You will note that in fifteen years, at age forty-nine, the total death benefit would be $152,728.

In the present inflationary climate with high taxes, tax-deferred annuities are particularly attractive.* These are sold by life-insurance companies, and having criticized the companies severely up to this point, I hasten to say that some of them do a good job in designing, marketing, and managing tax-deferred annuities. Perhaps the reason is that executives are waking up to reality. In this business, they are compelled to compete with other types of savings and investment products and services.

As a matter of fact, only within recent months (as this is written) have a few life-insurance companies recognized the plight of the consumer and begun actually offering a combined package of term insurance and tax-deferred annuities. This is certainly far superior for you to consider than buying cash-value life insurance or, as I have pointed out many times in this book, retaining such policies.

That brings up the matter of the kind of service one needs in estate planning. It is essential to have the services of

* See tables and explanation, pages 146–51.

an advisor whose income does not come from one life-insurance company, mutual-fund marketeer, promoter of real estate participations, or broker in stocks and bonds. What is needed is a money doctor; that's a new profession of experts who look after a family's financial health the way the general medical practitioner looks after the family's health. Just as the general practitioner refers patients to specialists, the money doctor does not depend entirely on his or her own expertise. She or he keeps up with trends and knows how to find the solution to any particular problem by a telephone call or consulting the current literature on the subject.

The ethics of a money doctor coincide with those of such professions as accounting, law, and medicine. The ethical doctor of money matters will make certain his or her financial prescriptions are relevant to the client's personal needs.

After all, once death insurance is paid off to the beneficiary, it is only money, and there are persons whose financial situations do not require the purchase or retention of death insurance. Their survivors may be adequately protected more cheaply by other means.

If your income or your assets are large enough, say a portfolio of a hundred thousand dollars, it may pay you to seek out a money doctor. In any case, once you find such an advisor and want her or him to carry out transactions for you at very modest commissions, it will pay to give this advisor all or virtually all the business you have on which he or she can make fees or commissions.

You won't find money doctors listed in the Yellow Pages. Most of them call themselves investment counselors and they serve larger personal-account clients or corporate clients. The easiest money doctor to find may be an independent insurance agent, the kind who sells both life and property-casualty insurance and annuities and who can also give advice on a variety of savings and investment opportunities.

Tailor-making your present and future financial security should not be taken likely. Honesty between you and your advisor or advisors is of paramount importance. By that I mean, don't get mixed up with a professional advisor who thinks commission dollars first and you second. On the other hand, you, too, must be honest. There is no point in telling your money doctor about money problems that don't exist now or may never exist. For example, if you have the ability to set aside fifteen hundred dollars a year for your financial security and that of your family in the event of your premature death, don't tell the money doctor that the figure is three times that amount. He or she will only come back to you with an elaborate plan that you can't possibly put into effect. The whole program ends up in the wastepaper basket and you and your family walk around naked, without proper financial security.

On the other hand, if you happen to have fifty thousand dollars at your disposal in cold, hard cash, you would be remiss in not telling your advisor about it. At this time, if the advisor knows his or her business, he or she will advise you to put most of this amount into a tax-deferred annuity where current interest at $12\frac{1}{4}$ percent can double your money in approximately six years.

> The following six illustrations show what happens to your money over a period of years at varied entry ages. This annuity contract, currently being issued by a New York State company, is one of the best in the industry today.

NO LOAD ANNUITY

			Single Premium : $50,000.00
Male, age 30			Normal Retirement Age : 60
Number of Deposits : 1			Optional Retirement Age : 65

Year	Projected Value—Tax Deferred *	Minimum Contingency Floor †	Guaranteed Value—Tax Deferred ‡	Value of Currently Taxable Program §
1	56,125.00	56,125.00	56,125.00	53,062.50
2	63,000.31	62,719.69	58,370.00	56,312.58
3	70,717.85	70,089.25	60,704.80	59,761.72
4	79,380.79	78,324.74	63,132.99	63,422.13
5	89,104.93	87.527.90	65,658.31	67,306.74
6	100,020.29	97,812.43	68,284.65	71,429.27
7	112,272.77	109,305.39	71,016.03	75,804.32
8	126,026.19	122,148.77	73,856.68	80,447.33
9	141,464.40	136,501.25	76,810.94	85,374.73
10	158,793.79	152,540.15	79,883.38	90,603.93
11	178,246.02	170,463.62	83,078.72	96,153.42
12	200,081.16	190,493.09	86,401.87	102,042.82
13	224,591.11	212,876.03	89,857.94	108,292.94
14	252,103.52	237,888.97	93,452.26	114,925.89
15	282,986.20	265,840.93	97,190.35	121,965.10
16	317,652.00	297,077.24	101,077.96	129,435.46
17	356,564.38	331,983.82	105,121.08	137,363.38
18	400,243.51	370,991.92	109,325.93	145,776.89
19	449,273.34	414,583.47	113,689.97	154,705.72
20	504,309.33	463,297.04	118,246.92	164,181.45

At Age

60	1,601,623.70	1,407,132.00	175,034.34	
65	2,854.251.50	2,452,293.80	212,956.04	

Monthly Income

60	12,825.80	11,268.31	1,099.22	
65	24,840.55	21,342.31	1,486.43	

* Projected values based upon current rate of 12.25% and settlement option rates, not guaranteed.
† If interest rate falls below 11.75% at any time during the first seven policy years, no surrender charges will be imposed.
‡ Assumes guaranteed interest rate of 12.25% first year and 4.00% thereafter.
§ Currently taxable assumes current rate for all years reduced by tax consequences of a 50% tax bracket.
Monthly income assumes life annuity with ten years certain.

NO LOAD ANNUITY

Male, age 35
Number of Deposits : 1

Single Premium : $50,000.00
Normal Retirement Age : 60
Optional Retirement Age : 65

Year	Projected Value—Tax Deferred *	Minimum Contingency Floor †	Guaranteed Value—Tax Deferred ‡	Value of Currently Taxable Program §
1	56,125.00	56,125.00	56,125.00	53,062.50
2	63,000.31	62,719.69	58,370.00	56,312.58
3	70,717.85	70,089.25	60,704.80	59,761.72
4	79,380.79	78,324.74	63,132.99	63,422.13
5	89,104.93	87,527.90	65,658.31	67,306.74
6	100,020.29	97,812.43	68,284.65	71,429.27
7	112,272.77	109,305.39	71,016.03	75,804.32
8	126,026.19	122,148.77	73,856.68	80,447.33
9	141,464.40	136,501.25	76,810.94	85,374.73
10	158,793.79	152,540.15	79,883.38	90,603.93
11	178,246.02	170,463.62	83,078.72	96,153.42
12	200,081.16	190,493.09	86,401.87	102,042.82
13	224,591.11	212,876.03	89,857.94	108,292.94
14	252,103.52	237,888.97	93,452.26	114,925.89
15	282,986.20	265,840.93	97,190.35	121,965.10
16	317,652.00	297,077.24	101,077.96	129,435.46
17	356,564.38	331,983.82	105,121.08	137,363.38
18	400,243.51	370,991.92	109,325.93	145,776.89
19	449,273.34	414,583.47	113,698.97	154,705.72
20	504,309.33	463,297.04	118,246.92	164,181.45

At Age

60	898,728.98	807,415.69	143,865.46	
65	1,601,623.70	1,407,132.00	175,034.34	

Monthly Income

60	7,197.02	6,465.78	903.48	
65	13,938.93	12,246.27	1,221.74	

*' Projected values based upon current rate of 12.25% and settlement option rates, not guaranteed.
† If interest rate falls below 11.75% at any time during the first seven policy years, no surrender charges will be imposed.
‡ Assumes guaranteed interest rate of 12.25% first year and 4.00% thereafter.
§ Currently taxable assumes current rate for all years reduced by tax consequences of a 50% tax bracket.
Monthly income assumes life annuity with ten years certain.

NO LOAD ANNUITY

		Single Premium : $50,000.00
Male, age 40		Normal Retirement Age : 60
Number of Deposits : 1		Optional Retirement Age : 65

Year	Projected Value—Tax Deferred *	Minimum Contingency Floor †	Guaranteed Value—Tax Deferred ‡	Value of Currently Taxable Program §
1	56,125.00	56,125.00	56,125.00	53,062.50
2	63,000.31	62,719.69	58,370.00	56,312.58
3	70,717.85	70,089.25	60,704.80	59,761.72
4	79,380.79	78,324.74	63,132.99	63,422.13
5	89,104.93	87,527.90	65,658.31	67,306.74
6	100,020.29	97,812.43	68,284.65	71,429.27
7	112,272.77	109,305.39	71,016.03	75,804.32
8	126,026.19	122,148.77	73,856.68	80,447.33
9	141,464.40	136,501.25	76,810.94	85,374.73
10	158,793.79	152,540.15	79,883.38	90,603.93
11	178,246.02	170,463.62	83,078.72	96,153.42
12	200,081.16	190,493.09	86,401.87	102,042.82
13	224,591.11	212,876.03	89,857.94	108,292.94
14	252,103.52	237,888.97	93,452.26	114,925.89
15	282,986.20	265,840.93	97,190.35	121,965.10
16	317,652.00	297,077.24	101,077.96	129,435.46
17	356,564.38	331,983.82	105,121.08	137,363.38
18	400,243.51	370,991.92	109,325.93	145,776.89
19	449,273.34	414,583.47	113,698.97	154,705.72
20	504,309.33	463,297.04	118,246.92	164,181.45

At Age				
60	504,309.33	463,297.04	118,246.92	
65	898,728.98	807,415.69	143,865.46	

Monthly Income				
60	4,038.51	3,710.08	742.59	
65	7,821.64	7,026.94	1,004.18	

* Projected values based upon current rate of 12.25% and settlement option rates, not guaranteed.

† If interest rate falls below 11.75% at any time during the first seven policy years, no surrender charges will be imposed.

‡ Assumes guaranteed interest rate of 12.25% first year and 4.00% thereafter.

§ Currently taxable assumes current rate for all years reduced by tax consequences of a 50% tax bracket.

Monthly income assumes life annuity with ten years certain.

NO LOAD ANNUITY

Male, age 45
Number of Deposits : 1

Single Premium : $50,000.00
Normal Retirement Age : 60
Optional Retirement Age : 65

Year	Projected Value—Tax Deferred *	Minimum Contingency Floor †	Guaranteed Value—Tax Deferred ‡	Value of Currently Taxable Program §
1	56,125.00	56,125.00	56,125.00	53,062.50
2	63,000.31	62,719.69	58,370.00	56,312.58
3	70,717.85	70,089.25	60,704.80	59,761.72
4	79,380.79	78,324.74	63,132.99	63,422.13
5	89,104.93	87,527.90	65,658.31	67,306.74
6	100,020.29	97,812.43	68,284.65	71,429.27
7	112,272.77	109,305.39	71,016.03	75,804.32
8	126,026.19	122,148.77	73,856.68	80,447.33
9	141,464.40	136,501.25	76,810.94	85,374.73
10	158,793.79	152,540.15	79,883.38	90,603.93
11	178,246.02	170,463.62	83,078.72	96,153.42
12	200,081.16	190,493.09	86,401.87	102,042.82
13	224,591.11	212,876.03	89,857.94	108,292.94
14	252,103.52	237,888.97	93,452.26	114,925.89
15	282,986.20	265,840.93	97,190.35	121,965.10
16	317,652.00	297,077.24	101,077.96	129,435.46
17	356,564.38	331,983.82	105,121.08	137,363.38
18	400,243.51	370,991.92	109,325.93	145,776.89
19	449,273.34	414,583.47	113,698.97	154,705.72
20	504,309.33	463,297.04	118,246.92	164,181.45

At Age

60	282,986.20	265,840.93	97,190.35	
65	504,309.33	463,297.04	118,246.92	

Monthly Income

60	2,226.15	2,128.85	610.36	
65	4,389.00	4,032.07	825.36	

* Projected values based upon current rate of 12.25% and settlement option rates, not guaranteed.
† If interest rate falls below 11.75% at any time during the first seven policy years, no surrender charges will be imposed.
‡ Assumes guaranteed interest rate of 12.25% first year and 4.00% thereafter.
§ Currently taxable assumes current rate for all years reduced by tax consequences of a 50% tax bracket.
Monthly income assumes life annuity with ten years certain.

NO LOAD ANNUITY

	Male, age 50		Single Premium : $50,000.00	
			Normal Retirement Age : 60	
	Number of Deposits : 1		Optional Retirement Age : 65	

Year	Projected Value—Tax Deferred *	Minimum Contingency Floor †	Guaranteed Value—Tax Deferred ‡	Value of Currently Taxable Program §
1	56,125.00	56,125.00	56,125.00	53,062.50
2	63,000.31	62,719.69	58,370.00	56,312.58
3	70,717.85	70,089.25	60,704.80	59,761.72
4	79,380.79	78,324.74	63,132.99	63,422.13
5	78,104.93	87,527.90	65,658.31	67,306.74
6	100,020.29	97,812.43	68,284.65	71,429.27
7	112,272.77	109,305.39	71,016.03	75,804.32
8	126,026.19	122,148.77	73,856.68	80,447.33
9	141,464.40	136,501.25	76,810.94	85,374.73
10	158,793.79	152,540.15	79,883.38	90,603.93
11	178,246.02	170,463.62	83,078.72	96,153.42
12	200,081.16	190,493.09	86,401.87	102,042.82
13	224,591.11	212,876.03	89,857.94	108,292.94
14	252,103.52	237,888.97	93,452.26	114,925.89
15	282,986.20	265,840.93	97,190.35	121,965.10
16	317,652.00	297,077.24	101,077.96	129,435.46
17	356,564.38	331,983.82	105,121.08	137,363.38
18	400,243.51	370,991.92	109,325.93	145,776.89
19	449,273.34	414,583.47	113,689.97	154,705.72
20	504,309.33	463,297.04	118,246.92	164,181.45

At Age

60	158,793.79	152,540.15	79,883.38	
65	282,986.20	265,840.93	97,190.35	

Monthly Income

60	1,271.62	1,221.54	501.67	
65	2,462.83	2,313.61	678.39	

* Projected values based upon current rate of 12.25% and settlement option rates, not guaranteed.

† If interest rate falls below 11.75% at any time during the first seven policy years, no surrender charges will be imposed.

‡ Assumes guaranteed interest rate of 12.25% first year and 4.00% thereafter.

§ Currently taxable assumes current rate for all years reduced by tax consequences of a 50% tax bracket.

Monthly income assumes life annuity with ten years certain.

NO LOAD ANNUITY

Male, age 55
Number of Deposits : 1

Single Premium : $50,000.00
Normal Retirement Age : 60
Optional Retirement Age : 65

Year	Projected Value—Tax Deferred *	Minimum Contingency Floor †	Guaranteed Value—Tax Deferred ‡	Value of Currently Taxable Program §
1	56,125.00	56,125.00	56,125.00	53,062.50
2	63,000.31	62,719.69	58,370.00	56,312.58
3	70,717.85	70,089.25	60,704.80	59,761.72
4	79,380.79	78,324.74	63,132.99	63,422.13
5	89,104.93	87,527.90	65,658.31	67,306.74
6	100,020.29	97,812.43	68,284.65	71,429.27
7	112,272.77	109,305.39	71,016.03	75,804.32
8	126,026.19	122,148.77	73,856.68	80,447.33
9	141,464.40	136,501.25	76,810.94	85,374.73
10	158,793.79	152,540.15	79,883.38	90,603.93
11	178,246.02	170,463.62	83,078.72	96,153.42
12	200,081.16	190,493.09	86,401.87	102,042.82
13	224,591.11	212,876.03	89,857.94	108,292.94
14	252,103.52	237,888.97	93,452.26	114,925.89
15	282,986.20	265,840.93	97,190.35	121,965.10
16	317,652.00	297,077.24	101,077.96	129,435.46
17	356,564.38	331,983.82	105,121.08	137,363.38
18	400,243.51	370,991.92	109,325.93	145,776.89
19	449,273.34	414,583.47	113,698.97	154,705.72
20	504,309.33	463,297.04	118,246.92	164,181.45
At Age				
60	89,104.93	87,527.90	65,658.31	
65	158,793.79	152,540.15	79,883.38	
Monthly Income				
60	713.55	700.92	412.33	
65	1,381.98	1,327.56	557.59	

* Projected values based upon current rate of 12.25% and settlement option rates, not guaranteed.
† If interest rate falls below 11.75% at any time during the first seven policy years, no surrender charges will be imposed.
‡ Assumes guaranteed interest rate of 12.25% first year and 4.00% thereafter.
§ Currently taxable assumes current rate for all years reduced by tax consequences of a 50% tax bracket.
Monthly income assumes life annuity with ten years certain.

To put things in the right order, let us consider term-insurance needs first. How much and what kind does the average couple need?

As an ideal minimum, most experts think a couple with one child should have $100,000 worth of term insurance during the prime years, $150,000 for two children, and an extra $25,000 for each additional child. Admittedly, a lot of people can afford the premiums for $100,000 to $200,000 worth of term coverage and meet their other obligations too.

There are many kinds of term insurance, but only three need be discussed.

Group term is the kind of insurance your employer buys for you. More than $1.42 trillion of it is in force in the United States, and if you have some of it, you naturally take that into consideration in buying other coverage. But the amount of an individual's group life insurance is generally not enough to satisfy family needs for death insurance, and as a rule, you lose it if you change employers.

Annual renewable term: the face amount of the policy is payable upon the death of the insured during the period for which the premium has been paid. The policy expires after one year unless renewed each year by the policyholder paying a revised annual premium, which is slightly higher in each succeeding year. A word of caution—always make sure that the policy you are buying gives you the privilege of renewing and converting without further medical examination. Your health today, unfortunately, may not assure your total insurability at all or at standard rates tomorrow. Renewable term can also be purchased for periods other than one year, such as a five-year renewable-convertible term policy. Depending on the age at issue, the average premium over the years can be more or less than that of the yearly renewable term.

Decreasing term can be the least expensive in premium cost. The reason is obvious. The face amount of the policy decreases each year and eventually becomes zero at the terminal age of the policy. Probably the best application for decreasing term insurance is to cover a business or home mortgage where the indebtedness declines each year and so your insurance may be permitted to decline.

One thing to make sure of is that you choose term insurance that is guaranteed to be renewable and convertible without further medical examination.

How much will it cost to provide the maximum death-insurance protection?

Many tables of the ranges of costs of term life insurance exist, but none are complete enough to give more than an indication of the possibilities. Here is a table of the range of prices developed from a typical company for $100,000 of five-year renewable and convertible term insurance at varying ages:

Age	Five-Year Renewable Convertible Term
25	$ 190
30	195
35	235
40	355
45	550
50	860
55	1,400
60	2,225
65	3,295

The above premiums are typical of policies issued by a stock life-insurance company. If you are a non-smoker you may enjoy an additional discount of about 20 percent.

As we now know, competition in the industry dictates that you get honest advice.

Quantity discounts are now prevalent in buying term insurance. Comparing the real cost and relative merits of five-year renewable term insurance and diminishing term is not easy. Before inflation became so acute, many persons considered diminishing term the best. Obviously, it is cheaper in the long run than five-year renewable term with the death benefit kept level at the maximum figure.

But inflation introduced a new element into the picture. During the earlier and middle period of life, inflation makes it incumbent on many couples to increase their insurance protection year by year instead of letting it slowly decrease. This makes the straight five-year renewable term policy more attractive than the diminishing policy. Actually, few buyers of five-year renewable keep the death benefit level. They raise or lower it each renewal according to changes in their protection needs, raising and lowering the premiums accordingly. If an increase is desirable, you had better make sure you maintain your health to be insurable. That is why I always recommend a big chunk of term insurance early. As you see, it is cheap enough and can protect your future insurability.

Since term life insurance is neither a savings nor an investment instrument but is only protection for survivors in case of untimely death, those who rely on it must make sensible savings and investment plans early. The inflationary climate of the 1970s has changed both savings and investment pictures. For example, bank accounts, which used to pay very low interest rates even though the interest was compounded, now pay eight to sixteen percent on some types of savings certificates.

Certificates in banks have become very popular and provide even the small saver with excellent interest-income returns. These certificates can be purchased for as short a period as six months.

Gold and silver, paintings, fine ceramics, antiques, postage stamps, and a variety of other art objects that investment counselors can call "collectibles" have grown enormously in value because of inflation, and the critical international political situation at the start of 1980 has accelerated this trend. Who would have expected to see gold hit $835 an ounce while the official U.S. mint price still is only about $40? Or the almost nine hundred percent rise in the price of silver in a year? But any collectible can be highly speculative.

Real estate, of course, has climbed out of sight because of inflation and because so many people need homes. Even some of the real estate investment trusts on which stockholders and banks lost billions of dollars in the early 1970s are starting to come back.

Although the progression of value in real estate has generally been true, I have seen countless persons lose their shirts in attempting to invest in this complicated field. Part-time venturers buy at the wrong time, only to suffer huge losses when they have to sell. It takes real skill to invest in real estate at any level, whether you are considering raw land, apartment houses, or office buildings.

Tax-exempt municipal bonds have also made something of a comeback, and new tax-exempt issues are paying better yields. I question, however, the advisability of investing in this area. Near financial collapse of so many cities such as New York, Cleveland, and Yonkers have caused me to wonder whether an investment in municipal bonds is prudent. After all, would you invest in any bond in any corporation where you knew the management was inept?

The trouble with all these investments is that except for bank deposits, where the Federal Deposit Insurance Corporation insures your account up to a hundred thousand dollars, they require unflagging study of the market trends and great expertise. You have to pick one or two fields and learn them yourself. No financial advisor could hope to keep up with them all.

That leaves annuities, mutual funds, and the stock market. In spite of their great popularity, I am not enthusiastic about mutual funds. I don't think their overall performance over the past twenty years has been good. Several published studies have shown that many mutual funds experience very little growth and have produced unsatisfactory income payment over periods of some years. A main reason for this is that most funds are heavily front-end loaded, to pay commissions and other selling expenses.

Also, the variety of mutual funds aimed at special purposes or tailored to fit some individual's idea of a magical formula is bewildering, so bewildering that the individual buyers of the shares have little chance of comprehending what they are buying.

As for the stock market, there are, indeed, many bargains to be found in it, but one may have to wait a long time to realize the gain. Prices on the New York Stock Exchange are not currently inflated as much as the general economy, so the present is a good time for making long-term investments in good stocks. It is not a good time to try for short-term profits by trading in shares.

On the other hand, prices of stocks listed only on some of the minor stock exchanges and in the over-the-counter market are inflated like the general economy, because institutions and private citizens are speculating in these markets. But whether investing or speculating, putting money in stocks takes up an awful lot of time and requires a tremendous amount of expert knowledge these days. What everyone hopes to find in the stock market is a special situation, a company with great growth prospects as yet undiscovered by the securities analysts and the speculators but fairly certain to be discovered soon. A relatively small investment in such a stock can run into a fortune.

But what happens to most investors is that they buy "glamour" stocks after the prices have already been run up, the way the gambling-casino shares skyrocketed in 1978 and early 1979. Then they hang on too long or not long enough and sell when all the rest of the panicky speculators are selling. Periodically, the glamour stocks have to tumble like houses of cards because their prices have run up far more than can be justified by any realistic earnings or expansion potential. Only the astute traders and investors buy and sell at the psychologically right times and make any money out of them.

As another word of caution: There have been too many headline stories of stockbrokers, even those connected with some of the more prestigious Wall Street houses, who took customers and their capital the way Grant took Virginia.

Once again, the greed of much of humanity must be watched carefully, particularly when investing in Wall Street. As mentioned earlier, the churning of funds to constantly earn commissions for the benefit of stockbrokers and to bleed customers is an ongoing problem.

Before going into the virtues of tax-deferred annuities, it may be well to make clear the difference between a tax deferment and a tax shelter. A tax deferment is simply a means of putting off paying taxes for some years. This serves two purposes: It enables an investment to grow faster by reinvesting the interest it earns, and it puts off payment of taxes on the interest until a time when one expects to be in a lower tax bracket than now. Additionally, taxes might come down through the workings of some miraculous reform in Washington. That has happened several times in our national history, although this generation might find that hard to believe.

The chance of a major change in taxation methods within the next decade makes tax-deferred annuities very, very attractive at this time. The possibility of going from the high-structured income-tax system of today to a value-added tax system is real. I predict that Congress will and must do something fast; otherwise the underground economy will become larger and larger and make taxation for the honest people more and more burdensome.

A tax shelter, on the other hand, is a means of avoiding or attempting to avoid taxes on certain income altogether and to create paper losses that can be used to offset taxes on other income. Since many persons who have some money to invest are solicited frequently by promoters of tax shelters, it may be well to say a little about them. Tax shelters are of two kinds, the legitimate and the dubious, and many of the dubious ones are plain attempted fraud. But the promoters still succeed in selling a lot of them and then disappearing, leaving the investors to hold the bag when the IRS cracks down. The dubious shelters are built around all sorts of schemes involving coal mining lands, old motion pictures and master phonograph records for which there is little demand, unsold stocks of newly printed books, fifth-rate paintings and other art objects, and bizarre mining prospects. Some of them involve charity-donation wrinkles.

They all have two common features—grossly inflated valuations of the property or merchandise involved and the creation of large amounts of nonrecourse debt, which the investor is told to take as a deduction against his or her other taxable income so as to get down into a much lower tax bracket. Nonrecourse debt is money the debtor owes on paper but is not really obligated to pay—the creditor has no legal recourse. Because the IRS takes a very jaundiced look at all deductions based on nonrecourse debt, the tax-shelter promoters try to disguise it as genuine "at risk" debt. The IRS is probably never really fooled by this, but a lot of tax returns with such deductions do get by, just by escaping being audited. When a taxpayer is caught at this kind of shenanigan, Uncle Sam can be quite nasty about it.

Legitimate tax shelters are those authorized by Congress for specific purposes, such as to encourage housing construction or exploration and drilling for oil and gas. Direct or participation investment in these activities can create unrealized losses that can be used to shelter other income from taxes. But investors must be very careful in purchasing participations in these activities, legitimate as they are. A number of them have been marketed by fast-buck artists who structured them with a grossly unfair division of profit and risk. The promoters skim off most of the potential profit in advance, and the investor is left with a small amount of profit and big risks. There are a lot of good legitimate real estate and petroleum tax-sheltered participations, but you must know how to find reputable dealers and operators, and investing in them usually takes quite a chunk of capital.

Annuities have been sold all over the world for many

years by life-insurance companies, but in the United States they have not been pushed hard simply because a life-insurance agent may make a much better commission by selling a whole-life cash-value insurance policy with the same premium.

Annuities pay much better yields than cash-value insurance for a variety of reasons, and their tax-deferment feature is a great help to many persons. Annuities come in several types, according to both the way one pays money into them and the way the annuitant gets it back with interest.

There are single-premium annuities on which the investor pays in a substantial lump sum either all at once or in two or three installments and then draws monthly payments from the fund and its accumulated earnings, starting either fairly soon or on retirement.

Then there is the flexible or installment annuity, to which the investor makes monthly or quarterly deposits over a period of years until the full amount has been paid.

Now, let's look at annuities in accordance with the way the money comes back to you.

The life-only annuity. The company guarantees to pay you a fixed monthly income, from the time agreed for payments to start until you die. But if you die after receiving only a few payments your widow and dependents get nothing. It's not a good plan.

Installment-refund annuity: Provides a refund to your beneficiary if you die before receiving enough payments to equal the deposits you have paid in plus the accumulated interest.

Life and ten or twenty years certain: If you die soon after starting to receive payments, the company will continue payments to your widow or beneficiary for the remainder of an agreed ten- or twenty-year period, but if you outlive this agreed period you continue to get payments.

Joint and survivor annuity: Once they start, the monthly income payments are made during the lifetimes of two persons, usually husband and wife. Under some plans, however, the payments to the survivor may be smaller than the payments made while both are living.

Regardless of the plan chosen, annuities have certain important benefit characteristics:

• The money you pay in comes out of your taxed income or your capital, hence can never again be subject to income tax. Only the interest it subsequently earns can be taxed.

• Taxes on this interest are deferred until the money comes back to you in the shape of monthly income payments or in a lump sum.

• If your contract designates someone other than yourself as annuitant when it is purchased, then no income tax is payable if you die before the period of return payments begins.

• An annuity account can be transferred from one life-insurance company to another without incurring any tax obligation on the interest funds. But such a transfer must be arranged by the new company or its agent. If you withdraw the funds yourself, even with the intent of buying a new annuity, the interest immediately becomes taxable.

As with life-insurance policies, there is an enormous variation in the prices insurance companies charge for similar annuities and there are huge differences in their terms and quality. Early in 1979, *Changing Times* magazine warned people to "Beware the hard sell annuity pitch." The article was sharply critical of the front-end-loaded tax-deferred an-

nuities being sold by many insurance companies and of the
tremendous discrepancies between the promises in the sales
pitches and the funds' actual performance.

No financially sophisticated person would buy a front-
end-loaded annuity. At least a half a dozen responsible companies now market a new kind of no-load single-premium
deferred annuity. Interest is paid on 100 percent of the principal from the date of issue of the policy. There are no off-
the-top reductions for commissions or overhead. The company
guarantees to return the entire principal at any time under
some circumstances. The interest rate is guaranteed for one
year of issue at the current rate, now 12.25 percent, and an
interest rate of at least 4 percent is guaranteed to matter how
bad business conditions get. At any time the interest rate
drops below 11.75 percent you can withdraw your entire
principal with interest from the fund without paying a surrender charge.

Regardless of the interest rate, you can withdraw up to
10 percent of your funds without paying a surrender charge,
and you need not pay taxes until 100 percent of your money
is returned. For larger withdrawals while the interest rate is
still above 11.75 percent you will have to pay surrender
charges for the first seven years. These charges start at 7 percent for the first year and drop to 1 percent in the seventh
year. After the seventh year there is no surrender charge;
thus, the fund seeks to guarantee both accumulation and
liquidity. (See tables on pages 163 and 164.)

The return-payment options are similar to those already
described. The company is able to avoid charging big front-
end fees because it is willing to wait years to reap its profit.
Meanwhile, it absorbs the sales commissions and other costs

NO LOAD ANNUITY

Single Premium : $50,000.00

Male Age 45   Normal Retirement Age : 60

Number of Withdrawals : 20   Optional Retirement Age : 65

Year	Withdrawal Amount *	Projected Value—Tax Deferred †
1	5,612.50	50,512.50
2	5,670.02	51,030.25
3	5,728.14	51,553.31
4	5,786.85	52,081.74
5	5,846.17	52,615.57
6	5,906.09	53,154.88
7	5,966.63	53,699.72
8	6,027.79	54,250.14
9	6,089.57	54,806.21
10	6,151.99	55,367.97
11	6,215.05	55,935.49
12	6,278.75	56,508.83
13	6,343.11	57,088.05
14	6,408.13	57,673.20
15	6,473.81	58,264.35
16	6,540.17	58,861.56
17	6,607.21	59,464.89
18	6,674.93	60,074.41
19	6,743.35	60,690.17
20	6,812.47	61,312.24

At Age

60	58,264.35
65	61,312.24

Monthly Income

60	466.58
65	533.60

* At end of year-and-a-day withdrawal date.

† End-of-year balance after withdrawal, projected values based upon current rates (12.25%), not guaranteed.

This illustration shows a ten percent withdrawal each year, indicating no surrender charge.

NO LOAD ANNUITY

Male Age 45
Number of Withdrawals : 20

Single Premium : $50,000.00
Normal Retirement Age : 60
Optional Retirement Age : 65

Year	Withdrawal Amount *	Excess Surrender Charge †	Projected Value—Tax Deferred ‡
1	6,173.75	33.67	49,917.58
2	6,163.57	28.01	49,840.89
3	6,154.10	22.37	49,769.92
4	6,145.34	16.75	49,704.63
5	6,137.27	11.15	49,645.01
6	6,129.91	5.57	49,591.03
7	6,123.25		49,542.68
8	6,117.28		49,494.38
9	6,111.31		49,446.12
10	6,105.36		49,397.91
11	6,099.40		49,349.75
12	6,093.46		49,301.63
13	6,087.51		49,253,57
14	6,081.58		49,205.54
15	6,075.65		49,157.57
16	6,069.73		49,109.64
17	6,063.81		49,061.76
18	6,057.90		49,013.92
19	6,051.99		48,966.13
20	6,046.09		48,918.39

At Age
60   49,157.57
65   48,918.39

Monthly Income
60   393.65
65   425.74

* At end of year-and-a-day withdrawal date.
† Excess surrender charge on amounts over the 10.00% annual withdrawal.
‡ End-of-year balance after withdrawal, projected values based upon current rates (12.25%), not guaranteed.
This illustration shows an eleven percent withdrawal each year. Note the small surrender charge the first six years.

NO LOAD ANNUITY

If you made an annual purchase payment of $5,000 at the beginning of each year, this is the way your accumulation values would grow:

End Contract Year	Guaranteed * Accumulation Value	Accumulation Value At Current Rates †
1	$ 5,613	$ 5,613
2	11,037	11,913
3	16,678	18,984
4	22,546	26,922
5	28,647	35,833
6	34,993	45,835
7	41,593	57,062
8	48,457	69,665
9	55,595	83,811
10	63,019	99,691
15	104,837	213,491
20	155,715	416,296
25	217,616	777,713
30	292,928	1,421,794
35	384,557	2,569,610

* Guaranteed Minimum Interest Rate—Years 2 to 10 .... 4.00%

Thereafter 4.00%

† Current Interest Rate 12.25%

The death benefit in any year is the accumulation value resulting from the application of current interest rates.

Illustrations involving current interest are not guaranteed but are shown solely to indicate results if current rates remain unchanged.

Note that if the purchase payment were made at times other than the beginning of the year, the values would differ from those shown.

gradually out of the margin between the interest it pays on the annuity funds and what it earns on them.

It is certain that the tax-deferred annuity with a relatively high-interest yield is the best and perhaps the only way many persons can be sure of offsetting inflation and providing a retirement income to supplement Social Security. The table on page 165 shows what can be expected from a good annuity in which you invest five thousand dollars annually (based on December 1980 figures).

A couple may accumulate an ultimate estate by hard work, intelligence, and good fortune over a reasonably long lifespan, but untimely death means that the immediate estate becomes the ultimate estate.

But remember, persons in the prime of life won't be drawing annuity-income payments for many years. In the meantime they need death insurance, lots of it at reasonable prices, and it's time to compel all the life-insurance companies to provide it.

Epilogue

THIS MANUSCRIPT IS BEING completed just three weeks after Ronald Reagan's resounding triumph at the polls over President Carter, and I look forward hopefully to the prospect of a genuine new era for our country, an era that will bring an end to the inflation that has been threatening to destroy America for nearly a decade and to the restoration of the proud United States dollar to a semblance of the health and prestige it enjoyed for generations.

I also hope to see the growth and power of big government curbed at last and some of the crippling shackles of overregulation struck from American industry and commerce so that our national productivity will start to grow rapidly again because the right incentives are held out once more to investors and to both white- and blue-collar workers.

I hope for a swift end to our humiliating posture before the whole world caused by our weakness, our vacillation, our ignorance, and the illusions we have nurtured in recent years about ourselves and other peoples.

Finally, I hope for an end of the deadly cynicism, vulgarity, and amoral permissiveness that have permeated our society for the past two decades, resulting in unbridled crime and corruption that would horrify all our forebears.

But none of us can really be so naive as to expect Ronald Reagan to bring about all these wholesome changes by himself. Nor can the men and women swept into political office with him do so. If we believe with Thomas Jefferson that that government governs best which governs least—and most of us do believe that—it is manifest that we must set the example for Washington, not Washington for us. We must pitch in and do the job on our own.

How do we do it?

The ability of the average American to control his or her financial affairs is increasingly limited by the intervention of insurance companies, particularly life companies, and their agents and the government into so much of their affairs. Insurance and the other financial activities so closely related to insurance influence almost every business or personal financial decision we make, and we cannot make good decisions if insurance companies and agents continue to abuse the trust we necessarily put in them.

Therefore, I want to close by pleading with everyone in the business of insurance to which I have devoted my life to put an end to this appalling abuse of the public's confidence and misuse of the people's money. We are counting on Ronald Reagan to at least make a dramatic start at halting the abuse of tax funds, but the abuses of business are just as evil, and the insurance industry should be among the first to clean house. They should use their vast financial resources (which in fact are really the people's money) to work with government to eliminate the cumulative decadence of recent decades.

We can set the necessary example for the government by living cheerful, honest, industrious, confident, and prudent lives. This book is about being prudent and thrifty and honest in our daily financial dealings so we can rebuild our self-confidence as individuals and as a nation and make our children and grandchildren proud of us.

Just in case there is any question in the reader's mind about my lengthy discussions in this book, I wish to say to my critics, who I know will be a minority of my readers, and my staunch supporters, who will be the majority, that I am totally against any individual, group of individuals, or an entire industry who will not give a fair shake to the average American.

For too long, too many have taken advantage of the ignorance of the insurance-buying public. The time is now to repent and mend the ways of those responsible so that everyone can obtain maximum death-insurance protection at minimum cost and build a nestegg for their survivors' financial security or their own during their twilight years.

The time is now for insurance executives in high places, primarily in the establishment companies, to stop influencing the regulatory authorities and give them an opportunity to regulate for all 225 million Americans.

Appendix: A Summary Quiz

Q: Why do you call it death insurance?

A: Because *life insurance* is a misnomer.

Q: What is death (life) insurance really good for?

A: Its only true function is financial protection for survivors if the insured dies.

Q: Does an unmarried person need death insurance?

A: Not unless he or she has dependents who would be seriously deprived by his or her death or unless he or she wishes to protect future insurability.

Q: Does a young husband need death insurance?

A: Absolutely.

Q: What kind does he need?

A: Term insurance, as much as he can afford to buy.

Q: How about whole-life insurance?

A: It costs too much and doesn't give necessary protection to survivors, as term insurance does.

Q: Aren't the cash values of whole-life insurance a good reason to buy it?

A: No. It's about the poorest possible way to save money.

Q: But doesn't cash-value life insurance force people to save who otherwise wouldn't save anything?

A: That's nonsense. Nearly everyone in America saves something, and most people save in ways that earn a lot more interest or dividends than a life-insurance policy earns.

Q: If husband and wife both have jobs, should both be insured?

A: Probably, but it's best to build up the amount of insurance on the major breadwinner's life first.

Q: How much term insurance does a young couple need?

A: Ideally, $100,000 if they have one child, $150,000 if they have two children, and $25,000 more for each additional child.

Q: Which is the best kind of term insurance—annual renewable or diminishing?

A: In the present inflationary climate, annual renewable is much better. It starts off at much cheaper premium rates, and you can increase the coverage or reduce it as your needs change, if you remain insurable.

Q: If the premium starts out low, won't it get bigger as I grow older?

A: Yes, but in your later years, when you need less protection, you can cut both the coverage and the premium.

Q: Is there much difference in the prices the various companies charge for term insurance?

A: The prices vary enormously. That's why you need a good independent agent.

Q: Is savings-bank term life insurance cheap?

A: Yes, but there are rather low limits on the amount of it one can buy. Some companies are now cheaper.

Q: What about group insurance?

A: Most people have some group life, and their employers pay for it. But the individual is seldom allotted enough group life to meet family needs, and of course, you normally lose it if you change employers.

Q: Should persons who are stuck with old cash-value life policies cash them in now and buy term insurance?

A: As a rule, yes. But be sure to buy the term insurance before you cash in the old policy. If anything went wrong, you could be left uninsured.

Q: What could go wrong?

A: You might fail the medical examination for the new policy, and in any case your agent could run into a lot of restrictive delays caused by state regulations on "replacing" old policies—delays that are unconscionable.

Q: Can a great deal be saved by surrendering cash-value insurance and buying term?

A: Indeed it can. You may get four or five times as much immediate death protection for less than half the premium you have been paying on the cash-value policy. And you should get a tidy sum of cash to put in the bank or invest some other way to earn a much higher return. It is possible at present to get interest rates of twelve percent and higher.

Q: If life insurance is a poor way to save, how should one save?

A: Savings banks, savings-and-loan associations, money-market funds, tax-exempt-bond funds, common stocks, mutual funds, and real estate participations, for example.

Q: Which of those is the best?

A: None of them. In the current inflationary climate, a no-load tax-deferred annuity seems the best and safest way to save.

Q: Are the others all bad?

A: Not at all. Some of them are quite good and safe.

Others, the ones that yield the most, are more risky, and the yields from frankly speculative investments such as gold and silver, some commodity futures, and art collectibles can be extremely high—they fluctuate up and down widely and can produce big losses at times.

Q: Who sells annuities?

A: Life-insurance companies primarily.

Q: How do you buy one?

A: You pay for it either in a single large lump-sum premium or in installments. If you buy while still young, you pay for it in monthly or quarterly installments. In either kind you start drawing monthly income payments out of the paid-up premium and the money it has earned at an agreed date.

Q: What does *tax-deferred annuity* mean?

A: The insurance company invests your premium, and it earns interest and dividends, but the income tax on those earnings is deferred until you start drawing it out in monthly payments at a time when you expect to be in a lower tax bracket.

Q: What will an annuity do for me?

A: Look at the charts on pages 146–51.

Q. Is it easy to choose an annuity?

A: Not really. Too many of them are heavily front-end loaded for agents' commissions, advertising, and other selling costs. Their performances vary a lot too. You probably need the help of a money doctor or a good independent insurance agent to pick one out.

Q: Why are front-end-loaded annuities bad?

A: Because they take so long to accumulate assets.

Q: How can companies that sell no-load annuities afford to do so?

A: Because they are willing to wait years to earn profits from these investments.

Q: How does the money doctor or independent insurance agent earn a living selling no-load annuities?

A: He or she generally gets a fee from the insurance company for placing your money with the company.

Q: Can one withdraw money from an annuity in an emergency?

A: As a rule, yes. But there may be a special charge for that.

Q: Are annuities portable? Can they be transferred from one company to another?

A: As a rule, yes.

Q: If term insurance and no-load annuities are so much better buys than cash-value insurance, why do the insurance companies continue to push the cash-value policies?

A: Because the companies make bigger profits on them and captive agents get bigger commissions on them.

Q: Can I get waiver of premium in case of illness and other special riders on term insurance?

A: Yes.

Q: Is cancer insurance a good idea?

A: No. It generally isn't worth what it costs.

Q: How about mail-order insurance?

A: It's usually fairly priced, considering that it is sold without medical examination, but beware of some "budget-priced" twenty-payment level-premium, level-death-benefit mail-order policies that are pitched hard in television and print advertising. They generally turn out to be grossly over-priced.

Q: Are policies issued by third party sponsorship, such

as alumni associations, professional associations, fraternal groups, and bank credit card offerings, a good buy?

A: It depends on from where they come—that is, who is sponsoring them, who the insurance company is, and the kind of deal engineered by the selling agent. Here, too, it may even pay you to pay a small fee to a money doctor to investigate the offering.

Q: Is credit life insurance necessary?

A: The federal government says it usually is not.

Q: Is it required by law?

A: Of course not, but banks and finance companies can require you to have it as a condition of granting a loan.

Q: Is it fairly priced?

A: No. Testimony before a senate committee showed it was priced at up to ten times as much as other term insurance. The insurance companies and the banks and finance companies that sell it for them make fantastic profits on it. They generally lend you the premium and charge interest on it.

Q: Can I shop around and buy my own credit life insurance or do I have to take what the bank is selling?

A: You can buy your own, and the bank must accept it. After all, credit life insurance should only be cheap term insurance.

Q: I have heard that partnerships and small corporations need business life insurance to tide them over when a partner or a key executive dies. Is this true?

A: Definitely.

Q: What kind of insurance would be best for this purpose?

A: The big establishment companies push whole life and cash values for business life-insurance problems, but many insurance people believe that term insurance does the job more cheaply and just as efficiently.

Q: What about major medical and health insurance?

A: Most people have some as part of a union or other employment contract, and older persons have Medicare. If you do not have either, you should buy individual policies of good benefits and low cost.

Q: Do persons over sixty-five really need death insurance?

A: It depends on how they are situated and whether they still have dependents. Many persons over sixty-five do not need death insurance, yet have poor policies for which they are paying too much. The premium could be better invested elsewhere.

Q: Should a person over sixty-five get rid of all his or her death insurance?

A: In most cases, the answer would be yes. After all, if you have $250,000 in the bank and in annuities and possibly other assets, why have death insurance? Insurance is nothing but money when eventually paid out, and if you have the money already, why pay premiums on insurance?

Q: Can death insurance help offset estate taxes?

A: Yes, but most married couples don't need it for that purpose because the marital exemption under the estate-tax law usually takes care of the problem.

Q: How frequently should a family review its death-insurance situation?

A: Inflation makes it desirable to review it more frequently than was thought necessary in the past. As a rule, term insurance has to be renewed every year or every five years anyway.

Q: Does recent competition in the insurance business dictate a more frequent review?

A: Yes, by all means. A review would probably indicate a change in policies or companies for your death-insurance protection to enable you to get maximum protection for minimum premiums.

Q: How does one get good advice on reviewing one's death-insurance situation?

A: Consult a money doctor or an independent insurance agent.

Q: How do you pay him or her?

A: Since his or her commissions on individual transactions are small, you can compensate such a person only by giving him or her a considerable amount of business—death insurance, an annuity, fire insurance, automobile insurance, and business insurance—and letting him or her handle some other investment transactions for modest fees.

Q: How much faith can one put in life-insurance-company advertising?

A: The life-insurance industry is no different from any industry that uses advertising techniques. Madison Avenue techniques are even used by political candidates. A lot of it must be taken with big grains of salt.